THE
RULES
OF
PEOPLE

Pearson

At Pearson, we have a simple mission: to help people make more of their lives through learning.

We combine innovative learning technology with trusted content and educational expertise to provide engaging and effective learning experiences that serve people wherever and whenever they are learning.

From classroom to boardroom, our curriculum materials, digital learning tools and testing programmes help to educate millions of people worldwide – more than any other private enterprise.

Every day our work helps learning flourish, and wherever learning flourishes, so do people.

To learn more, please visit us at **www.pearson.com/uk**

THE
RULES
OF
PEOPLE

A personal code for getting
the best from everyone

RICHARD TEMPLAR

Pearson

Harlow, England • London • New York • Boston • San Francisco • Toronto • Sydney
Dubai • Singapore • Hong Kong • Tokyo • Seoul • Taipei • New Delhi
Cape Town • São Paulo • Mexico City • Madrid • Amsterdam • Munich • Paris • Milan

PEARSON EDUCATION LIMITED
KAO Two, KAO Park
Harlow CM17 9NA
United Kingdom
Tel: +44 (0)1279 623623
Web: www.pearson.com/uk

First edition published 2017 (print and electronic)

ISBN: 978-1-292-19163-8 (print)
      978-1-292-19164-5 (PDF)
      978-1-292-19165-2 (ePub)

British Library Cataloguing-in-Publication Data
A catalogue record for the print edition is available from the British Library

Library of Congress Cataloging-in-Publication Data
A catalog record for the print edition is available from the Library of Congress

10 9 8 7 6 5 4 3 2 1
21 20 19 18 17

Cover des...

Print editi...
Print editi...

Contents

Helping people 66

Getting them on your side 104

Difficult people 166

Introduction

Over the years I've written down many Rules based on my observations of what behaviour is most likely to lead to a happy and successful life. Several hundred Rules, in fact, across this whole series of books. Each one of them outlines some way you can behave, something you can do, a way you can look at things, which will go some way to improving your life. Roll them all up together and the potential for getting the best out of life is huge.

However, I'll be the first to admit that there is one tiny flaw in this: other people. It doesn't matter how effectively you assert control over your own actions and reactions, how minutely you plan your own life – other people can always come along and chuck a spanner in your freshly oiled and smooth-running works. And there's nothing you can do about other people's behaviour. Or is there?

Well, that's where this book comes in. Because actually, you'd be surprised just how much you can do to encourage other people to behave in ways which will benefit both you and them. I'm sure you've realised through your life that the best times are the ones when everyone is pulling together, working in harmony, feeling a spirit of co-operation. Unless you're a sociopath – which I doubt if you've picked up this book – you're happier when the people around you are happy. Not rocket science, is it?

So it follows that the more you can do to make everyone else's life better, not just your own, the easier and more enjoyable your own life becomes. The skill is in creating happy people around you. Yes, even that grumpy colleague, or your stressy sister, or your critical college tutor could be a bit less grumpy or stressy or picky if you knew how to handle them. Of course you can't wave a magic wand and make all their troubles vanish, but you can at least make the time they spend around you more pleasant for everyone.

Many years ago I worked with a guy who was really difficult. I hated going into the office in the mornings. He didn't like me any more than I liked him, and while we both remained civil and well-behaved, the animosity was obvious. Eventually someone sensible banged our heads together, and I resolved to give him a second chance. Fortunately he did the same thing with me.

Now, the only thing that changed at this point was our behaviour. I was still the same person and so was he. However, those little changes in behaviour made so much difference that we saw a completely new side to each other. And – almost as if we'd been acting out some corny movie – we became firm friends, keeping closely in touch even after we'd both moved on to other jobs and other parts of the country.

It taught me just how much difference my own behaviour makes to the way other people act around me. And in the decades since, I've observed countless times – in others as well as myself – how one person modifying their behaviour can influence the people they interact with.

We all deal with lots of very different people in a normal day – different in terms of their own personality, and in terms of their relationship with us. There are people you encounter at work or college, who you want straightforward dealings with that don't cause hassle or unpleasantness. Then there's your family, who you care deeply about and can't really feel good unless they're all broadly OK. And then there are your friends, who you hang out with because you like being together, but sometimes you worry about them, and some of them can be tricky at times. And there are all the people you encounter in between – the shopkeeper you always stop for a natter with, the neighbour who is mostly friendly but doesn't like your cat, the client you're trying to close a deal with, the chap who organises your running club, your dentist, the customers who come into your shop, your child's teacher . . . these diverse people will all make your life easier if you can do the same for them.

All those different people having different lives – how are you supposed to know how to get the best out of them all? The answer is that they're not as different as you might think. Not in the ways that matter. The guidelines, principles, strategies – the Rules – that you need to know will help your relationships with everyone.

The first section of this book is all about understanding people: what makes us all tick. We're all pretty similar underneath, and if you understand people in general you're a long way to understanding the specific people you come across every day. I've also included a section on how to help people, because we all want the people around us to feel good. Sometimes we love them so much it hurts if they're in any trouble, sometimes we want to get the best out of them, and most times we'd rather other people were happier than not. It makes it easier to sleep at night if we've done our best for the people we've met that day.

Of course, a lot of your dealings will be with people who you'd rather were for you than against you. You want to get them on your side because they can give you support, or make your life easier, or improve your sales, or go along with your decisions. There are lots of ways to encourage people to throw in their lot on your side, and to feel good about it. And that's what you want. We Rules players aren't interested in manipulating or coercing people. We want them on our side willingly. In fact we don't want sides at all. Just everyone in agreement.

Having said all that, there's no denying that some people can be just plain tricky. Maybe they've had a tough day, maybe they've had a tough life, maybe they have no excuse. Whatever the reason, it helps to know the best way to handle them, so I've concluded the book with some useful Rules for getting the best out of some of your more challenging colleagues, family and friends.

All the central Rules are here, but of course there will always be other useful guidelines for dealing with people. If you have any favourites of your own, you can contact me via my Facebook page (below). I can't promise always to find time to respond, but I can promise you that I'll read your post with interest.

Richard Templar

www.facebook.com/richardtemplar

UNDERSTANDING PEOPLE

When everyone is happy and pulling together, we all benefit. You want to get the best out of people, for their benefit and yours, and you also want to be able to help and support them as well as possible. The two go hand in hand really. So to get the best, you have to know what makes them tick.

You wouldn't expect to be able to fix your car when it breaks down without knowing what goes on under the bonnet. It might have been something really simple, but without a grasp of basic mechanics you can't fix it, can't expect it to get you home. A simple understanding about how the internal combustion engine works, though, and you've a decent chance of making it to your destination.

Just so, even a rudimentary knowledge of what makes people work will mean you can get what you need from them, and help them along the way too. This first group of Rules sets out principles of human behaviour which will be useful in dealing with other people. These are the underlying factors which cause people to behave as they do, and which can give you clues to persuading them to behave differently where their current style works against either you or them, or both.

I've included a few Rules at the end of this section about helping your own child once they become a teenager, because I've found a lot of parents feel they flounder at this stage. They can see their almost-adult offspring need support but don't feel confident about how to give it. Mind you, all the Rules apply to teenagers you know who aren't your own child, and a lot of them are echoed in other relationships too.

There's nothing tricky or scientific here – I'm not clever enough for that. These are just basic observations, many of which you will recognise once you think about them.

Understanding helps

We all have a backstory. It explains why we behave as we do. OK, it doesn't always justify it, but at least it's a reason for our behaviour. Of course, no one else ever knows all the details and complexities of your backstory like you do, but lots of people get the gist.

There'll be a reason why certain things make you feel more anxious, stressed, excited, cynical, depressed, relaxed, angry, confident than other people do. It might be genetic, it might be because of bad past experiences, or according to Freud it might all be down to your parents. Friends might say that you shouldn't stress so much about this, or be so suspicious about that, or be too laid back, or shout so much. But they don't understand – if they'd been to the same school as you, or lived through the poverty you have, or had siblings like yours, or worked for your last boss, they'd realise why you behave that way.

Listen, this is true of everyone. There's no one on the planet who isn't shaped by their personal experiences. So when your colleague snaps at you, or your friend lets you down, or your partner forgets your birthday, just remember there's always a reason. It might be a rubbish reason, but there's a reason.

And I'm telling you this because if you can understand the reason, it makes it easier to deal with other people's negative behaviour. Even if you can't change the way they act, you'll find it slightly easier to take if you get the reasons behind it. And often simply because you're prepared to understand, they can let go of being defensive and decide to change their behaviour.

Suppose your boss is always stressy whenever there's a risk of getting behind schedule, whether it's a prestige project or just an internal lunch meeting. It's not your fault, and you don't appreciate them taking out their stress on you. But what if you knew – or even just suspected – that their father was a strict disciplinarian who hated lateness? Or in their last job they missed out on promotion because they missed a crucial deadline? Doesn't that make you feel a weensy bit more sympathetic? Wouldn't you like to help a bit? Good. Then make sure that you're always in good time, and if anything has to run up to the wire, keep your boss fully in the picture well in advance about when everything will happen, and spell out why it means you won't overrun. There now. Your boss will be less stressed and less stressy with you. Isn't that better?

Let's be clear – I'm not excusing bad behaviour.[1] Of course no one should take their stress out on someone who doesn't deserve it. Or their anger, their anxiety, their insecurity or anything else. But it happens. This is about helping you to cope when you're on the receiving end of it. I'm not asking you to understand the other person's motivations for their sake, but for yours.

THERE'S NO ONE ON THE PLANET WHOSE PERSONAL EXPERIENCES AND MAKE-UP DON'T SHAPE THEIR BEHAVIOUR

---

[1] Theirs or yours.

No one has to be like you

I used to sit next to someone at work who liked their desk to be unnecessarily, pointlessly, excruciatingly tidy. That's how I saw it anyway. All the files lined up, neat little coaster to put a coffee mug down on, every pen and hole puncher and paperclip exactly in place. It followed through to the way he worked too. Everything had to be filed the instant he finished using it, all notes had to be made in the right colour pen, every email colour-coded and archived, detailed to-do lists all marked with codes to indicate priority, urgency and importance.

It drove me mad. He couldn't do anything impulsively, or change direction in the middle of a task, or be spontaneous about following up ideas. Or cope with me dropping an untidy file on top of his perfect array of squared-up paperwork. I used to think it was absurd that he was stifling his own creativity and hamstringing his ability to be flexible.

But...As usual, I had to concede eventually that there was a but, and it was this. If there was a sudden emergency, guess who could always find the relevant email before anyone else? Who could be relied on to notice if the rest of us forgot some vital component of a task? Who could organise any event or project with superhuman efficiency? Who was always on time at every meeting with all the paperwork, and spare copies in case people like me had left theirs on their desks?

If I'm completely honest, for a long time I looked down on my colleague because he couldn't generate ideas like I could, or get other departments to put themselves out for ours, or act spontaneously. But it wasn't his precisely ordered desk that stopped him doing those things. He just wasn't that kind of person. The desk was the most obvious indicator of who he was, and of his own particular skill set, which was very different from mine. And – I came to realise – at least as valuable as mine. Just different.

Almost all of us are guilty at times of thinking our way is best. And that people who are different from us are wrong – or at least less right than us. I remember at the age of about 12 staying over at a friend's house and discovering that his family used a different brand of toothpaste from ours. I thought they were really weird – obviously our toothpaste was the best brand, or we wouldn't use it. So why weren't they using it too?

Like all this stuff, I know you know it really. It's just easy to forget sometimes. When other people are driving us up the wall, it's so much simpler to criticise them for being stupid or irrational or unreasonable than to consider that maybe their behaviour is actually quite legitimate but doesn't happen to suit us. However, if you want to get the best out of people – for you as well as for them – you have to be firm with yourself about acknowledging that just because you don't like something, it doesn't mean it's wrong. Once I finally accepted that my colleague was never going to have a messy desk like mine, and that actually that was OK, it was much easier to like him and appreciate him.

> # JUST BECAUSE YOU DON'T LIKE SOMETHING, DOESN'T MEAN IT'S WRONG

RULE 3

People hear what they want to hear

A teacher friend of mine tells me it can be really hard getting through to a student that they're studying the wrong subject if they want good grades – this subject just isn't their forté and they're not going to do well in it. Sometimes, she tells me, she has to be quite brutal just to get them to listen to what she's saying.

The fact is that people are programmed to pick out the things that they want to hear, and ignore the things they don't – programmed to such a degree they're unaware they're doing it. But if you want to get people on your side, and get their co-operation, you need to understand that if they don't want to hear something, it will take a lot more effort from you to get your point across.

It's human nature – no use getting frustrated by it. You just need to take it into account. Whether you're telling your boss that the report you're working on can't be completed to their deadline, or telling your sister that you can't all go on holiday together as one huge family, have your antennae tuned to whether they've really taken on board what you're saying. If you suspect they haven't – if they're arguing with the facts, or still talking just as they were before you put them straight – explain it more clearly ('The next data drop isn't until the twenty-second of the month, which means we can't start crunching the numbers until then') and, if they still don't seem convinced, ask them questions ('Can we guesstimate the figures so we don't need the latest data?'). Questions will force them to think about the problem, so it makes them engage with the problem they're sidestepping.

And don't blither about. Make your words concise, clear, specific, blunt. Don't tell your boss, 'The problem is that, well, you know, it's looking tricky for the end of the month. I mean, the data drop is very close to the deadline, and it's a lot of work, so...hard to see how we can get it done in time.' Nope, you have to say, 'I'm afraid the report won't be done for the end of the month. I can get it to you on fifth of next month.' Put it in writing too if you can.

And why don't they want to hear it anyway? Does it make extra work for them? Or will they have to break unpleasant news to someone else? Or it means they can't have the outcome they wanted? Or it messes up their plans? Or it involves change and they don't like change? If you can identify their mental block, it's obviously going to make it easier to overcome. At the very least, it will help get your point across: 'I know it feels as if we're letting Mum down, but we simply can't afford a holiday this year.'

Listen, you need to get through to this person sooner rather than later. If your boss just isn't going to have that report by the end of the month, or there's no way to have a big family holiday this year, you need to get this across. The longer it takes for them to grasp it, the worse it will be all round. And the other person will say things like, 'I know you said it was difficult, but I didn't realise it was impossible...' or 'Why didn't you tell me sooner?' and you'll want to tear your hair out because you did tell them sooner. Only they didn't hear it.

Oh, and before you ask, yes, this does apply to you as well. You hear what you want to hear too. Never hurts to be aware of it.

> # DON'T BLITHER ABOUT. MAKE YOUR WORDS CONCISE, CLEAR, SPECIFIC, BLUNT

RULE 4

People believe what they want to believe

I read something interesting recently. Researchers took two groups of people with opposing political views on a particular topic, and gave them each statistics and other relevant data – hard facts – about it. They discovered that regardless of which side of the argument they were on, people believed that the facts supported their view.

What we believe isn't just about objective facts. It's about our whole outlook on the world, which is a complicated mix of how we were raised, our past experiences, what our friends believe, who we want to impress, how we see ourselves. The whole concept of 'belief' is often applied to spirituality because it has as much to do with faith as with facts. And that's something you can't argue with, however much you might like to.

When was the last time you had a heated political debate with someone who ended up saying, 'Actually, fair point. You're quite right. I've changed my mind'? It almost never happens. Because we all debate the facts; but they're just a tiny part of what makes up our beliefs. For example, a racist and a non-racist arguing with each other will quote loads of statistics about the effect of immigration on the jobs market, or inner-city crime rates, but the data aren't the real reason they hold their view, so that's not likely to change their minds.

What really happens is that we form our beliefs on the basis of a gut feeling, and then we post-rationalise it – we look for facts that back up what we've already decided to believe. Only we're not aware of the process, so we fool ourselves into thinking our view makes more logical sense than the opposing one.

That's why there's really no point discussing politics or religion with other people (apart from people who already agree with you, of course). Problem is, words, facts, statistics – the tools you have to hand when you're debating – will never change people's beliefs.

Frequently, nothing you can do will change them, and you're wasting your time. That doesn't mean it's impossible for someone to change what they believe. But the thing that will change them is an immersive experience. They have to live it for themselves – you can't do it for them.

You might have changed your own beliefs over the years, either suddenly or almost imperceptibly. So look back at why you stopped voting Conservative and started voting socialist, or went from being an atheist to a Muslim, or stopped approving of private education, or came to think that abortion should be available on demand, or decided that maybe peanut butter and jam do go together.

How often would you say the change was the result of a discussion with someone who disagreed with your opinion at the time? I'll bet the answer is almost never. It will be because you lived somewhere new, or got to know a group of people whose situation influenced you, or changed your personal circumstances, or did the kind of job that taught you to see the world differently. In other words, no one changed your beliefs for you. You changed them by yourself in response to your own life experiences.

Just remember that next time you're in a heated debate with someone who holds a view that you consider to be stupid or illogical or untenable in some way. I'm not suggesting you shouldn't stand up for what you believe in. Just be realistic about the chances of getting the other person to change their mind.

> **THEY HAVE TO LIVE IT FOR THEMSELVES – YOU CAN'T DO IT FOR THEM**

RULE 5

Your attitude influences their response

People don't operate in a vacuum. We're social animals and we need interaction. We play off each other. We spark each other's imaginations. Our emotional and mental needs are often met not by what we communicate, but by the way we communicate it.

This isn't big news; it's a reminder that communication relies on both (or all) the people involved to be effective. When the person you're talking to appears not to be listening, you feel angry, or belittled, or frustrated. You know this, but do you always stop to think about the effect you're having on other people?

If you want your relationships to be rewarding and productive – which you do – you need to acknowledge your own contribution to each conversation and interaction. For example, if you look like you're expecting a fight, you'll get a fight. If you act like you're a pushover, people will take advantage of you. If you appear confident, other people will trust you to do the job properly.

Any time you want a particular response or reaction from someone, think about what you put into the communication in order to get what you want out of it. This might be a one-off challenge – maybe to get your boss to give you a chance to prove yourself – or it might be an ongoing pattern you want to break. So if your friend always talks you into doing things you don't really want to, think about what it is you do or say that makes your friend put pressure on you. Have you got in the habit of giving up before you start, and saying no when you know you'll say yes eventually? If you want things to change, you'll need to work on that. Next time, be prepared to be assertive and mean it when you say no.

I've known people who get far less than they deserve out of meetings because they sound hesitant when they speak. It makes them seem unsure, inexperienced, incapable. Especially if they use an upward inflection at the end of sentences which sounds as if they're even questioning themselves. No one in the room is conscious of why they react as they do – they just don't feel convinced by the speaker. The very same person, making the very same recommendations, might get an entirely different response if they spoke with conviction and confidence.

Obvious as this may seem, just observe how many people fail to grasp it. All around you, you'll see people who say they don't want to row with their kids, but then aggressively nag or criticise and wonder why their kids answer back. You'll see people who want to persuade a meeting round to their way of thinking, but go into the room defensive and belligerent, which is never going to help.

It's not as obvious as it seems when it's *you* talking. So next time a conversation doesn't go the way you want it to, try reflecting on how you approached it. I'm not saying it's your fault, I'm not saying you do it every time. But if you want things to go your way, think about it.

> # IF YOU LOOK LIKE YOU'RE EXPECTING A FIGHT, YOU'LL GET A FIGHT

RULE 6

Remember your first impression

I remember someone I took on at work. She ticked all the right boxes – she was friendly, outgoing, qualified, experienced, keen. All the characteristics I was looking for. There was something about her that niggled, mind you. Just a vague feeling in the back of my mind that she was a tricky, demanding type. There was absolutely nothing concrete to back it up though, and she was by far the most suitable applicant for the job, so she got it.

Her first day at work she asked to change desks. There was another free desk anyway – the one she was asking to switch to – so I agreed. Slightly reluctantly, because again I had that niggle that she was asking as a kind of test of the boundaries, but she had a logical reason to prefer it so we went ahead. Everything went fine for several months, and she was indeed extremely good at the job. I pretty much forgot my niggling doubts from when I first met her.

And then she asked to cut down to four days a week. Again, she had a good reason (her mother was very ill and needed extra care) and it was true she could fit the same number of hours into four longer days. So I agreed, even though it wasn't a role that suited flexi-working, but let her know it wasn't ideal and not to ask to reduce her hours further. She was appreciative and said that was absolutely fine.

For about six months. And then she asked to reduce her hours and cut down to three days a week. This was simply unworkable – I needed her in the office – so I said sorry but no. And she walked out. Didn't work her notice, just collected up her stuff and left, telling me how impossible I was to work for. Left me completely in the lurch.

Those first impressions you have of people, they're so often right. For ages you can think you were mistaken and then, all of a sudden, you find you were spot on. Now, actually, I got 18 months excellent work out of my erstwhile employee, and although she left me in a mess when she went, I got it sorted pretty fast and it was probably worth it overall. So with hindsight I might still have given her the job.

However, it's a reminder not to ignore your first impressions, and not to forget them. Like me, you might not choose to act on them and that's fine – just go into the situation with your eyes open. And if things start to get tricky later, have that first gut feeling still in mind. Don't forget that sense you couldn't quite trust someone, or the intuition that told you they wouldn't stick around, or the instinctive doubt about their reliability.

It doesn't matter if your concerns never come to anything. No one's the wiser. But if things start to go wrong you can check back to your initial gut response.

Incidentally, it can also work the other way round. Sometimes you get a sense that someone unprepossessing is actually really loyal, or resilient, or generous underneath. Remember that too, if you ever need to call on those qualities in the future.

> FOR AGES YOU CAN THINK YOU WERE MISTAKEN AND THEN, ALL OF A SUDDEN, YOU FIND YOU WERE SPOT ON

People are tribal

Everyone wants to belong – it's human nature. But what do we belong to? Actually, we all belong to lots of tribes and groups, some bigger, some smaller. Some close, some more distant. You belong to your family, your village or borough, your city or region, your country and so on. You also belong to your school, or the company you work for, or your local health club, or your social media group.

We're loyal to our tribe – that's kind of what defines it as a tribe. It's a group we feel loyalty towards because we feel we belong to it, we're part of it. But of course, that sense of loyalty and belonging is stronger towards some of our tribes than others. Most of us feel a deep bond with our family, then strong but less so to our local community, then our region, then our country and so on. If you work in an office, you probably feel part of the company, but your strongest tie is to your department, then your section or branch, then your regional division and so forth. Sometimes you can break these down further: immediate family, extended family, broader family group (cousins and so on).

That's all well and good, until there's a conflict of interests between these groups. Suppose what's best for your organisation isn't best for your department? What if the best thing for your country as a whole is going to have an adverse effect on your town? Well then, you're likely to put the closer, stronger tribal bond first. Or at least, that's what you'll want to do – you might let your head overrule your heart but most people don't.

This is at the root of a lot of global problems. On a national level you could call it patriotism, or you could call it protectionism, depending on your perspective. However much we'd like everyone in the world to be happy, if we feel our own happiness is threatened by a move towards the greater good, it's hard to vote for the greater good.

This is the human condition. We're a social species, and our instinct is to show the strongest bond and protection towards the tightest, closest social group. That's not to say that an action or a vote for our own personal tribe is always the right thing to do, but that you have to expect people to favour their own tribe. If you want them to support your interests, you need to find a way to get them to feel part of your tribe.

That's what supermarkets do with 'loyalty card' schemes. They want you to feel loyal to them so you keep shopping with them. They want you to consider yourself part of the Tesco tribe or the Wal-Mart tribe or whatever it happens to be. Mind you, people aren't stupid either, and a card alone doesn't cut it with most of us. But canny businesses will find other ways to make us feel we belong.

I'm not saying this is right or wrong, I'm saying that you have to factor it in when you want to understand – or influence – how people behave. It's often at the root of a small action by a friend or colleague, and also behind global political movements, which can be driven by a collective fear that a tribe is under threat. For example, the UK vote to leave the EU is ultimately about tribal politics, and a stronger bond to the home nation than the home continent. I'm not getting into politics here, just looking behind it.

> **IF WE FEEL OUR OWN HAPPINESS IS THREATENED BY A MOVE TOWARDS THE GREATER GOOD, IT'S HARD TO VOTE FOR THE GREATER GOOD**

RULE 8

Everyone wants to feel valued

Low self-esteem is behind a huge amount of unhappiness and, indeed, mental illness. A lot of behaviour that drives you mad in other people, from bullying to control freakery, can be fed or even caused by poor self-esteem.

The word self-esteem has become used much more frequently in recent years. When I was young, people used a different term to mean the same thing – self-worth. In some ways I prefer the old-fashioned term because its meaning is much more obvious. It's about seeing yourself as being of value.

This sense of having value is something that everyone needs to be comfortable in their own skin. Some of us struggle with it more than others, and we all have times in our lives when it comes easier or harder. For example, your parents might have felt they were valued, important, useful when they were bringing up a family, but once the kids have left home and they retire, they might start wondering what use they are to anybody.

Some teenagers struggle with this because, especially in the West, they aren't always expected to make a contribution – either to society or just to the family – so it's hard for them to feel they have value. It's the teenagers who have Saturday jobs, and do chores round the home, whose self-esteem benefits.

You're not responsible for anyone else's self-esteem – so long as you're not undermining it – but it's useful to understand that this is a feeling everyone needs. Even your overbearing, charismatic, confident colleague. Maybe they already have a healthy sense of self-worth, but if it was undermined and taken away, they'd suffer badly.

A lot of people don't recognise when they are valued, especially if they've learnt, for whatever reason, to doubt their worth. Most of us need to be told to be really sure of it. So if you want to make someone feel good about themselves, let them know when they've been helpful, useful, valuable. A thank you is OK, a bit more than a thank you is better: 'Thanks. I don't know how you did that so quickly, but it's made my day a whole lot easier.' The more specific you can be about what they did, the more genuine and believable it is. That's why a mere thanks is better than nothing, but only just.

You'll also find that people are far more likely to co-operate with you if doing so makes them feel good about themselves. That's a win/win. So make sure you give people credit when they've added value. They'll want more of that good feeling, and you'll get the help you need plus the feeling you've added a few drops to someone's self-esteem bucket. Why wouldn't you want that?

> # A THANK YOU IS OK, A BIT MORE THAN A THANK YOU IS BETTER

They only tease you if they like you

Some people hate being teased, because it makes them feel criticised in some way. We generally tease people about something that could be construed as a fault or a flaw, which therefore appears to carry a degree of criticism with it. Maybe the fact they have a tendency to be late for things, or the fact they bang on too much about a particular favourite topic, or the way they dress. Sometimes we even turn positives into negatives and tease someone for being predictably efficient or always impeccably turned out.

That's what teasing is – gently making fun of someone about any trait that we particularly associate with them, dressed up jokingly as a negative in order to make it humorous.

There is a line you can cross here into bullying, of course – which can be a different way of making fun of someone and drawing attention to perceived flaws. But bullying is a very different thing.

The difference is this. People bully in order to make the other person feel uncomfortable in some way. It's not meant to feel good to be on the receiving end. However, teasing is an affectionate thing, and we only tease people we like. Its intention is to bring the teaser and the teasee[2] together by sharing laughter, or at least humour. It's a positive, feel good thing. Think about the people you tease – family, friends, favourite work colleagues. We don't tease people we dislike. We might make snarky remarks (well, we might if we weren't Rules players) but teasing is affectionate so we save it for people we feel affection for.

I've known plenty of people who didn't like being teased until they grasped this fact. Once you recognise it as a gesture of affection,

---

[2] No idea if that's a word. It is now.

suddenly being teased becomes positive. What's more, because we like the people we tease, we don't use teasing to highlight genuine failings. We wouldn't want the person to think maybe we meant what we were saying. Suppose you get really wound up by a friend who cancels arrangements at the last minute far too often. You wouldn't tease them because you wouldn't want to risk upsetting them. If you wanted to address it, you'd approach them about it seriously.

This means you can be confident that anything you get teased about isn't true, or it wouldn't be suitable material for teasing. So if your colleagues tease you about always being hung-over when you come into work, either it's not really true or it genuinely amuses them. If it bothered them, they'd sit you down for a quiet word about it.

Of course, just occasionally someone may inadvertently hit a raw nerve. In that case it's fine to explain that you'd prefer them not to tease you for that particular trait. If they hold you in affection, they should be happy to accede.

ONCE YOU RECOGNISE IT AS
A GESTURE OF AFFECTION,
SUDDENLY BEING TEASED
BECOMES POSITIVE

. . . but banter isn't teasing

You can argue semantics with me on this one. What one person classifies as banter, the next person might term teasing. Or bullying. Either way, the last Rule was obviously about affectionate and harmless ribbing, while this one is about the territory between what I call teasing and something that is clearly bullying. I'm using banter to mean something that upsets the other person. However, the most obvious feature of this grey area is that the perpetrators have no intent to upset the other person (whereas bullying is sustained and deliberate victimisation). And yet they do.

One of the interesting things about bullying is that it's very hard to assess objectively. Someone at work might say something to you as a jokey put-down, and you might find it amusing and enjoy finding a witty retort. But the same comment from the same person to one of your colleagues might be deeply upsetting. In a scenario like this, it's hard to argue that the person making the remark is a bully. They didn't intend to upset anyone, and yet . . . and yet . . . well, they have upset someone. Because it's not just what you say, or even how you say it, but also who you say it to.

This is the grey area I mean by banter. And it shouldn't happen, clearly, because someone has been upset and that's never alright. But I didn't call it banter when the comment was made to you – that was affectionate teasing and it's fine. So your workmate is allowed to make this comment to you – but not to their other colleague. Same comment, same commenter, different rules. Confusing, isn't it? The thing is, we all have different experiences and different views of the world. There will be a reason why one person is hurt by a remark that another person would shrug off. Of course, you don't know what that reason is, or indeed how they'll react before it happens.

It means that when you make this kind of jokey, teasing remark, you have to be alert to the other person's response. If you've evidently overstepped the mark and you get the message and don't repeat it, that's the best you can do. If you continue with such remarks, you're straying dangerously close to bullying territory. Yep, you're saying something in the knowledge it will upset the other person. There's no getting round that being bullying. Similarly, anyone – even if they're a friend of yours – who persists with comments once they know they are upsetting someone, is becoming a bully.

The worst cases of banter tend to be among groups of friends, where sustained banter about one of the group can help to cement the 'tribe'. Everyone jokes about how short so-and-so is, for example, because that's become part of the behaviour that identifies you as a member of the tribe. Often almost everyone in the group gets picked on for some characteristic or other. Meanwhile so-and-so wants to stay in the tribe, but actually hates being ribbed about their height. They feel bullied, but don't feel they can say so.

The banter within groups can become a serious form of bullying, where the victim can't express their hurt because this would weaken their membership of the tribe. Yet they don't feel able to leave the tribe. As Rules players, of course, we need to make sure this isn't happening among our friends, never join in, and do our best to put a stop to it. Not easy, but we have to try.

> # ANYONE WHO PERSISTS WITH COMMENTS, ONCE THEY KNOW THEY ARE UPSETTING SOMEONE, IS BECOMING A BULLY

RULE 11

Everyone else is insecure too

Ever had to give a presentation at work? It can be terrifying. Maybe not every time, but they can have a lot hanging on them in terms of meeting targets, impressing the boss, and maybe having an impact on more senior management too. You feel anxious and worried, of course you do, because it matters and nothing must go wrong.

Other people seem to give slick, polished performances and look as confident as if they were just making themselves a sandwich or going for a walk. Nothing to it – done it countless times before. Why would anything go wrong?

It's all an act, you know. Inside, they feel just as nervous as you do. And on the outside, you probably look as calm and self-possessed as them. Why wouldn't they be worried? Their presentation matters as much as yours, so it would be strange if they didn't worry.

Yes, I know there are a few very lucky people out there who are such confident and experienced public speakers that they really don't get anxious. But far fewer than you think. And a handful who don't get as nervous as you do – again, far fewer than you think. Even if you hyperventilate wildly and think you're going to pass out, you're in a much bigger minority than you realise.

And here's another thing. Those people who really do take presenting in their stride – all of them get insecure and nervous in other situations. *Everyone* does. Not all to the same degree, but everyone recognises that feeling. Maybe it's brought on by going to parties, or having to cook for people, or swimming, or job interviews, or committing to a relationship, or spiders, or hospitals, or having sex. We are all a product of our experiences, and no one has had a life devoid of the kind of experiences that lead to feelings of insecurity, worry and anxiety. No one.

If you want to understand people (and that's the way to have the most productive relationships), you need to know that however confident someone appears, they'll have their own insecurities hidden away somewhere. You might never see them, but you can be sure they're there. Sometimes someone you consider to be really together will behave in a totally unexpected way. And maybe it will be because deep down they're just feeling small and anxious. I know people who have a tendency to get angry if they feel under pressure to do something that seems a bit scary to them. Even if they put the pressure on themselves. Some people clam up, or get defensive, or come up with all sorts of spurious arguments against a course of action. They either don't recognise or don't want to admit to their insecurity, but that's what's behind it. So be on the lookout for hidden insecurities, and be kind when you spot them. You know how it feels.

> MAYBE DEEP DOWN THEY'RE JUST FEELING SMALL AND ANXIOUS

Spots don't change

Each of us is a unique concoction of our genes, our upbringing, our experiences. None of these are things we can change. And together these ingredients make us the extraordinary, unique people we are today.

Now, I don't know if you're much of a cook, but if you were to put together eggs, self-raising flour, butter and sugar, you'd pretty much get a cake of some sort.[3] There's not a lot you can do about that. If you'd wanted an omelette, say, you shouldn't have put the sugar in (or indeed the flour, and most of the butter). If you're working with a preset group of ingredients, you don't have much room for manoeuvre.

This is just as true of people. They are what they are. A given set of genes, along with a particular history of experiences. Most of us don't spend a lot of time thinking about what made us who we are, so we don't have much control over how we behave, react, feel, cope, function.

It's easy to look at other people and think they 'shouldn't' behave a certain way, but actually they haven't got much choice. You might think you'd act differently, and you'd probably be right, because your raw ingredients are different. If you started out with no flour or sugar, and you've even got a nice bit of cheese, you could produce a lovely omelette. But they can't.

I'm not saying you and I can't learn to change if we want to, but that's because we can choose to expose ourselves to circumstances that enable us to do that. Or, of course, maybe we can't make that choice right now – we'd need the right ingredients to be able to change.

---

[3] You will need to bake them. I just mention that in case you're really, really not a cook.

Let's not get into a philosophical debate about free will and determinism (interesting though that is). This is about other people. And the Rule is that other people don't have the same choices as you (if they even have any choices) about how they behave. So you can't expect them just to magic themselves into a different person because it suits you. Whether your partner can't cope with commitment, or your boss never delegates properly, or your child is hopeless with money, or your dad doesn't know how to express affection, or your sister always chooses to criticise rather than praise – you'll drive yourself mad trying to make them who you think they should be. The sooner you accept them as they are, the easier it will be for you.

Your boss can't delegate because of an almost infinitely complex array of past experiences and innate character, and unless they *choose* to change, it just won't happen. Maybe it won't even if they really want to. You're banging your head against a brick wall. If your relationship can only work if your partner changes their attitude to commitment, then I'm afraid it can't work, because their attitude is a part of them. Of course, you could maybe choose to change your need for commitment... or could you?

> ## YOU CAN'T EXPECT THEM JUST TO MAGIC THEMSELVES INTO A DIFFERENT PERSON BECAUSE IT SUITS YOU

RULE 13

Behaviour isn't character

This Rule follows on from the last, and might help if the last Rule seemed depressingly unhopeful. While it's true that people can't change their character, they can – sometimes – change their behaviour.

It won't help if you think this is a cure-all, because it isn't. There are times when we just aren't able to adapt, especially when we're being asked to adapt in a way that runs counter to our underlying character. So don't read this Rule and think, 'Well that's OK then. My overcritical sister can behave differently, and stop voicing her criticism.' In theory she could, but she might struggle. For whatever reason (her past, her genes), she believes it's the right thing to do. She might think it's just being honest, or that it's for your own good – in which case why would she stop? The really important thing here, however, is that even if she did stop verbalising her criticism, she'd still be thinking it. That's the bit you have no chance of changing.

Sometimes, getting someone to change their behaviour is enough. You might not care about their underlying character. If you can get your boss to delegate, that's the battle won. Who cares how they feel about it underneath? Not you, anyway. But don't be surprised when a really important project comes along and they go back to their old ways, because they didn't change deep down, and their old fear of delegating was still lurking beneath and is right back when the stakes are high.

Suppose your partner is infuriatingly messy. You can never find anything in the kitchen because nothing gets put away in the same place twice. You might be able to persuade them that there would be fewer arguments if they behaved tidily, even if it's not really them. They might struggle, and it might be harder for them if they're in a hurry, or stressed, or cooking something complicated. But it could work.

You might have spotted the silver lining in all of this. The people around you are a product of their experiences, and when they change their behaviour, they'll have new experiences to match. Your partner will find out what it's like to cook in a tidy, organised kitchen. Your boss will learn how it feels to be able to offload some of their work. This might, over time, have an effect on their character. It might help them to appreciate order, or to loosen up. These are things that may have seemed scary in the past but they're now learning that it's OK, and even beneficial.

Obviously they might not. If anything happens to reinforce your boss's old fear of delegating, they may get worse and not better. Similarly, your partner might re-encounter those old feelings of being constrained and strictured which they always kicked against. You can't assume that a change of behaviour will lead to a change of character. But if it doesn't, nothing else you can do will. (Although maybe you could try to change your behaviour and become more tolerant?)

SOMETIMES, GETTING SOMEONE TO CHANGE THEIR BEHAVIOUR IS ENOUGH

Other people's relationships are a mystery

No, really. It's hard to describe how weird and wonderful other people's relationships can look from the outside, quite possibly including your own. Some very happy-looking relationships can be unhappy or even abusive below the surface, while some of the most worrying relationships might actually be giving both partners exactly what they need. Even that is fraught – some people have an emotional need for something that might not be in their best interests. So however it looks to you, you just have no idea what goes on behind closed doors. Even if – especially if – one of the two people involved takes you into their confidence.

Let me give you just a few examples, all of them based on couples I have known:

- They never have a cross word, and appear happy. But both hate conflict so are hiding a mass of unresolved problems they don't know how to address.

- They argue constantly, but are both passionate people who enjoy releasing their feelings, and enjoy making up afterwards. They're actually really happy together.

- They argue constantly, and it works well for one of them. The other one is deeply unhappy but every time they raise it, there's another argument.

- One of them is very controlling. The other is compliant, but enjoys the feeling of being able to rely wholly on their partner.

- One complains constantly that the other is useless. But when the other one tries to contribute, the first one carps and criticises and tells them how useless they are.

These are bound to be only a miniscule sample, and hugely oversimplified, because every relationship is unique. The point, however, is the same – don't ever try to judge someone else's relationship.

This kind of hidden agenda can apply to relationships other than romantic partners, parents and their adult children being the most obvious example. Mind you, these are different because you're stuck with your parents/children (unless you take the very drastic measure of cutting them out completely). But then some romantic partners are stuck with each other, unable for whatever reason to separate.

Listen, all relationships take two people. A relationship is a thing we create together. We might be happy, or we might have chosen to be resigned, or compliant, or aggressive. But somewhere along the line, that choice has worked for us or we wouldn't have made it. Just remember that when you're trying to grasp what two of your friends could possibly be doing together.

If you have a difficult relationship with a parent, by the way, the odds will have been stacked unfairly in their favour for the first couple of decades of your relationship, but even so you won't respond exactly as your siblings do (or would if you had them). In fact you might respond very differently. Somehow you've found a way of co-existing up to now. If it's not what you want, you'll have to take positive action if you want it to change.

> # EVERY RELATIONSHIP
> # IS UNIQUE

Big words are there to impress you

Have you ever listened to someone talk who is both clever and confident in their own knowledge? Politicians, top business people, successful actors, authors, comedians, sports people? People who aren't trying to prove anything, who are happy in their skin? Almost always they come across as approachable, easy to talk to, easy to understand. That's because they have no need for any of the barriers some people inadvertently put up, in order to prove something to the rest of the world.

Any time you see someone trying to impress you in any way, it's a pretty good sign they feel insecure and are trying to compensate. They think you'll judge them if they show what they believe to be their true colours, so they try extra hard to cover them up. For example, people with a chip on their shoulder about coming from an impoverished background often flaunt money when they have it, to make a point about not being poor.

The key things here are that *they* are uncomfortable about their background, and they are expecting you to judge them for it. In fact you might not care about their background, but it's all about their perception. Others might be proud to have pulled themselves up by their bootstraps, but this person is a teensy bit ashamed of where they come from.

Another good example of this is people who use long words and sentences to make themselves look well educated and erudite. They think (wrongly I hope) that you'll look down on them if you know their education wasn't great. But they reckon they can fool you into thinking they're clever by using convoluted sentences and complicated words. Or rather, into thinking they're cleverer than they think they are. See, it's all about their perception again. It has absolutely nothing to do with what you actually think.

In fact, if we judge people's use of language at all, it's by their clarity, not their ability to overcomplicate. That's why people with nothing to prove don't try to impress – they don't need to. People who use big words might think they're impressing us, but they only impress themselves.

It's a shame, because if someone really does come from a background of poverty, or has been unlucky enough to be poorly educated, they deserve our support. But the people I'm talking about here expect us to judge them harshly, even though you and I would do no such thing. So it's worth being tolerant of the symptom, and recognising the underlying cause, next time you encounter someone who is trying a bit too hard to impress.

> **PEOPLE WITH NOTHING TO PROVE DON'T TRY TO IMPRESS – THEY DON'T NEED TO**

Confrontation can be scary

There's almost never any need for outright confrontation. In fact, never at all so long as both of you are behaving like adults.

The trouble is, some people are so anxious about raising the things they are unhappy about that they'd rather leave a problem unresolved. That's the safe option, isn't it? At least that way they don't risk a stand-up argument. They're afraid that talking about the problem will lead to slammed doors and hurt feelings and horrible atmospheres.

I remember a friend telling me, distraught, about a row over a big family get-together that had really upset her. She'd discovered there were differing opinions about whether everyone should go out for a meal or stay in (no one wanted to cook, but not everyone could afford a meal out). However, she hadn't said anything because she didn't want to kick off an argument. Then her brother found out not only that there was a problem, but also that she'd known about it for ages and said nothing. He was furious with her.

Ironically, if only my friend hadn't dreaded confrontation, but instead had managed to raise the problem in an honest, straightforward way, so it could be discussed, it wouldn't have happened. People who put avoiding confrontations too high up their priority list will sometimes inadvertently create bigger rows by doing so. Maybe they also sometimes avoid them altogether, but there's usually a cost. If something needs resolving and you don't resolve it, it'll still be there. Unresolved.

You need to know who these people are around you. Which of your colleagues, family, friends would rather bottle up frustrations and worries than voice them, just in case you get angry. Maybe you are a bit inclined to fly off the handle, or maybe their fear is irrational and you're really not the type. Doesn't matter much whether they're right. Your problem is that you don't know what's bugging them if they won't tell you – and vice-versa. And until it's resolved, they won't be as productive, relaxed, trusting, honest, co-operative as you want them to be.

I hope you've sussed the way round this by now. Yep, you're going to have to broach the subject yourself. Tricky, of course, because you don't actually know exactly what's bugging them. Also because if you seem remotely confrontational, you know they'll clam up. But don't worry, there's a classic approach that will work.

Their problem is also yours. So talk to them about *your* problem. And tell them 'When you do this, I feel that...' For example, 'When you go quiet, I feel you're angry with me', or 'When you don't tell me what's happening, I feel you don't trust me'. This is a really neutral, rational, non-personalised and non-argumentative way to kick off the conversation, and signals that you're not interested in having a row, you just want to get to the bottom of your problem. Remember, it's their problem too, and they also want to fix it. Now you've handed them a way to do that, the conversation can be friendly and productive. And who knows, maybe over time they'll even learn how to raise issues with you themselves.

> # IF SOMETHING NEEDS RESOLVING AND YOU DON'T RESOLVE IT, IT'LL STILL BE THERE. UNRESOLVED.

RULE 17

People feel nervous because they care

What makes you anxious – giving a big speech? Starting in a new job? Waiting to run onto the pitch for an important game? Broaching a difficult conversation with someone? Going into an exam (or getting the results)?

When you're really nervous, you can shake, sweat, struggle to string words together, your heart rate increases and you can feel weak. What's more, your head is full of clamouring thoughts, usually centred on what could go wrong and how terrible it would be if it did. You imagine all kinds of humiliating or catastrophic scenarios.

Because it would be terrible if it went wrong, wouldn't it? I mean, you'd really mind. A lot. That's the reason you feel nervous. It seems obvious, but you probably aren't thinking about the reason for it because you're too busy trying to calm down and stop thinking about failure.

Now then. Suppose you were about to go into an exam you didn't care about. You're only doing it because you've been told you have to, but it's a subject you're not interested in, and you don't need to pass in order to do anything that matters to you. You didn't bother studying because you don't care what happens – the whole exercise seems pointless. Are you feeling nervous? Of course not, because you don't care.

So when you encounter someone who seems really nervous, just remember that it's really important to them to do well. Whether they're a new member of the sports team, or a colleague about to give a presentation, or someone asking you for help or advice – their nerves show you that they care. And that's always a good thing. Shows they have integrity and drive and want to succeed.

So be sensitive. Be reassuring. Be kind. Don't tell them not to be nervous – they'll just worry that they're disappointing you, or their nerves are getting in the way. No, don't tell them. *Help* them not to be nervous. Show them how to achieve what they want, tell them you're glad they're nervous because it shows they care.

The best cure for nerves is confidence. And you achieve that by knowing what you're doing. If you go onto that pitch knowing you're the best player there, or walk out on stage confident that you could deliver your speech in your sleep, or sit down to an exam having revised for it so thoroughly you know you can answer any question – well, then you'll be far less nervous. So when someone seems anxious around you, remind them how much they know, or run through their moves or their presentation with them, or reassure them that they're not expected to know how to do the job on their first day.

BE SENSITIVE. BE REASSURING.
BE KIND

RULE 18

Angry people are sad people

I knew someone who reacted to every perceived slight from other people with anger. He'd tell me about something that had happened that made him feel bad, and he'd say, 'I felt frustrated and angry', or 'I felt sad and angry', or 'I felt hurt and angry', or 'I felt embarrassed and angry'. Always angry, whatever other emotions were going on. It seemed to be his default setting.

Some people are just given to it. All of us have flashes of anger from time to time, but this is about those people who seem to spend a lot of their lives angry. It bubbles so close to the surface that it takes very little for it to erupt in another outburst.

Think about how you feel when you get angry. You become intimidating so it makes you feel, at least to some degree, more powerful. It's a positive driving action, not a passive one. And this is the key to understanding angry people. Their anger is a cover for an emotion that makes them feel weak and helpless. They hate that feeling, so they cover it up with a response that makes them feel powerful and in control – anger.

We've all done it. Your child runs across the road without looking and almost gets hit by a car. You scoop them up into a big hug and then instinctively get angry with them. What you really feel is fear,[4] but that's a helpless and unbearable emotion, so you mask it with anger, which makes you feel powerful and in control. It makes perfect sense.

Routinely angry people are doing this most of the time instead of just occasionally. I can't tell you why some vulnerable people cope in this way and others don't – we're all different and there will be countless factors which determine any given person's

---

[4] Or, in this instance, what one of my children likes to call 'hindsight worry'.

response. For example, it's not unusual in men who were told as kids that 'big boys don't cry' and have found a less vulnerable way to express their sadness. What I can tell you is that angry people are sad – or hurt or scared or ashamed, all of which are pretty sad states too.

It's also helpful to know that their outbursts will be sparked by situations in which they feel powerless in some way. If they feel slighted, or embarrassed, or think they've been ignored, or are fearful of failure or of retribution, these are the times you can expect them to regain a feeling of power and control by lashing out.

There may be very little you can do about the friend, relative, co-worker, colleague you know who is so angry. The root causes probably go back a long way. But just understanding that they're deeply sad on some level might help you to cope a bit better with being around them. They may not come across as a sympathetic person, but they probably deserve sympathy nonetheless.

> # IT'S A POSITIVE DRIVING ACTION, NOT A PASSIVE ONE

Crying isn't always sad

This Rule is the inverse of the last one, and just as Rule 18 is perhaps more common in men than women, you may encounter this more often in women.

Lots of people cry because they're sad, as you'd expect, but for some people that's not the only reason. Crying is a kind of all-purpose expression of emotion anyway – after all, we even do it when we're relieved or overjoyed or laughing or full of love. Of course, you can generally tell when someone's crying is an expression of negative emotion. Just not necessarily sadness.

One of the most common instances of this is women who have been brought up to feel that anger somehow isn't ladylike (no, I don't get it either). But if you've had this drummed into you from early childhood, it's not surprising if you've learnt to cry when you feel angry (because girls are 'allowed' to do that).

No wonder this response will generally accompany you into adulthood. So you can see that if you encounter someone sobbing and looking sad – while unbeknownst to you actually feeling angry – they may not appreciate you saying 'Aaah . . . there, there', and making sympathetic sadness noises. No one wants to hear that when they're feeling furious. If you get a response that doesn't stack up when you show sympathy with someone's sadness, consider whether maybe you're sympathising with the wrong emotion.

Crying and anger aren't the only emotions that can mask others. To be honest, it is pretty confusing trying to read other people's emotions, especially if you don't know them particularly well. It can be pretty straightforward, but we all bowl emotional googlies at times, and they can be hard to read and respond to.

Another example that stands out is people who use humour to cover up fear or embarrassment. Sometimes they're best left alone – clearly they want to hide their feelings, so why add to their embarrassment by drawing attention to it? But other times they might really want help, if they're trying to conceal a real and significant fear, for example.

So the moral is, don't assume the emotion you can see is the real one. Probably it is, but if other things don't add up, consider whether something more subtle is going on. If you want to help, and good for you, you need to get to the bottom of the real problem and it's probably simplest to ask what's going on.

> **DON'T ASSUME THE EMOTION YOU CAN SEE IS THE REAL ONE**

RULE 20

Some people just don't think

I recall a colleague of mine being deeply hurt and upset once because he'd been excluded from a meeting he felt he ought to have been asked to attend. He spent ages worrying about why he'd been omitted, not liking to ask the Chair because he didn't want to come across as petulant, or needy, or something. We all told him not to worry about it, but he got himself into quite a state. Anyway, come the meeting, about five minutes in, the Chair asked why he wasn't there. We explained he hadn't been included, and of course it turned out there was some technical reason why he wasn't on the Chair's email group, only she hadn't noticed.

The thing my workmate had never considered, in all his fretting about why he wasn't wanted, was that it was simply an accident. He assumed the Chair had thought through who was invited, but in fact she simply hadn't thought at all. That was a possibility he, ironically, didn't think of.

It's surprising how often this kind of thing happens. This Rule is titled 'Some people just don't think', but in some ways I could have called it 'All of us don't think sometimes'. Not very grammatical but perhaps more accurate, because we all do this from time to time. How often do you catch yourself about to miss someone out, or fix a date for a party completely forgetting that one of your close friends told you they couldn't make that date? It's so easy, and yet it's often the last explanation we think of when we're on the receiving end.

Sometimes it's nothing but an understandable error with unexpected consequences, as was the case with my colleague. At other times it's what we term 'thoughtless' – in other words, the person really should have been thinking, and was out of order in not making sure they got things right. Nevertheless, it's still unintentional, and thoughtlessness is not malicious.

I once made someone a birthday cake completely forgetting they were gluten intolerant. Stupid, stupid thing to do and I could have kicked myself a dozen times over. The worst of it was, for some reason they thought I'd done it on purpose and got upset. It took me ages to explain that I simply hadn't thought about it. They believed me in the end but I was still furious with myself because obviously I felt I should have remembered.

When you're trying to understand someone's motivation for doing something that doesn't seem to make sense, always consider the possibility that they simply didn't think. It's so much easier to take than being deliberately snubbed or offended or excluded or riled or upset, and so often the true explanation.

THOUGHTLESSNESS IS NOT MALICIOUS

Square pegs don't fit in round holes

A wise man I used to work with pointed out to me once that just about everyone in the world falls into one of two groups when it comes to work. We all have a significant preference for either project-based or routine-based work. Personally, I like a project. That's one of the reasons I write books. I see a thing through from start to finish and then I start fresh on something else. I've worked in companies where I've set up departments, and then moved on to something else. I get bored and frustrated just doing the same thing day in, day out. At least, that's my perspective.

Other people, of course, enjoy the security of a job which continues in the same vein indefinitely – with the occasional promotion – and they find variety in the detail which I can't see, because I'm always rushing on to the next thing. The world is full of jobs of both kinds, at every level, from school leaver to senior management. And the world needs both kinds of people.

Strangely, this isn't something I hear careers advisers talking to people about. But if you apply for a routine-based job when you're a project person, or vice versa, you won't really be happy doing it. More people should point this out to teenagers, and to anyone looking for a new career.

This is just one example of the kind of holes you have to match up with the right pegs. There are plenty of other walks of life where people can end up trying to squeeze into holes that don't fit them. Some parents just aren't cut out to stay home all day with the kids. Some managers are great organisers but aren't leaders of people. Some people are really happy working alone, others need lots of social interaction.

Here's my point: don't flog a dead horse. I'm all for people learning to adapt their behaviour when it's helpful to do so – as you know – but this isn't about behaviour. This is about a much deeper part of our inherent personality, and you won't change it. So don't ask square people in round holes to become rounder, because they can't. Whether it's your child who will never be a natural at learning languages, or your partner who can't be happy if they give up work for the next 18 years, or your team member who gets bored with routine work, or your non-conformist friend who hates working in big institutions, their options are to be unhappy or to find themselves a nice square hole to hang out in.

Some people spend decades trying to escape from round holes. Some never manage it. But the only solution that works is to change the hole, because a square peg will always be a square peg. You need to recognise when the people around you are stuck in the wrong holes. Maybe your child could do well in German or Mandarin if they put in a bit of effort, but maybe languages will never be their thing. Perhaps your partner could be content staying at home with the kids if they had time for a hobby on the side, but perhaps they can't be happy without a proper job. Listen to them properly, and talk it through, and be open to the possibility that they simply don't fit where they are.

So resist the temptation to ask your square partner, child, colleague or friend to change shape, and accept that it's not in their power. Then you can support them in the search for a nice square hole to snuggle into.

> # THE ONLY SOLUTION THAT WORKS IS TO CHANGE THE HOLE, BECAUSE A SQUARE PEG WILL ALWAYS BE A SQUARE PEG

Wild and wacky isn't always fun

Some people lead wild lives. I don't just mean interesting. Quite often I don't *even* mean interesting. I mean lots of sex and drugs and rock 'n' roll. Always out partying and full of stories afterwards – if they can remember anything – of the crazy things they did and how drunk they were and how much fun it was, and how many times they were sick. But have you noticed that sometimes they almost have an air of desperation, as though they need to convince themselves how fantastic their life is? They're weaving a narrative for their own benefit more than yours. Creating a mythology of their life that they can believe in.

That's because spending your whole time drunk or stoned or waking up in strangers' houses – or beds – isn't actually much fun. The confusion, the hangovers, the drunken arguments... doesn't really sound great, does it?

Listen, I'm not suggesting that you should never have fun, go wild, let your hair down a bit. Every so often it's good for you, but everything in moderation, eh? These people, though, just don't seem to understand that you can have too much of a good thing.

Or maybe they do understand it deep down, and they just don't want to hear it. A lot of people who behave this way do it because they're trying to distract themselves from some part of their lives or themselves that they can't cope with. They might seem boorish and loud – or even fun and exciting – but inside they're lost and vulnerable.

That means that they're not worth envying, because you probably wouldn't want to be them really. They also deserve sympathy rather than approbation, because they're fighting demons we wouldn't want.

Think about the people you know who fit this wild and wacky description. Perhaps one or two on the fringes might simply enjoy a good night out rather more than the rest of us. But when you consider some of them, and especially the most hard-bitten, committed, wild and drunken people, it's not hard to believe that they're constantly on the run from their demons, unable to stand still and just enjoy life in case the demons catch up. So they cavort and spin and dance and take refuge in drink or even drugs, simply to drown out the sound of the demons' footsteps coming after them, and forget what it is they're trying to escape from. There may not be much you can do for them, but you could try feeling sympathy rather than envy, and don't assume they're fine just because they claim to be.

Actor and notorious hellraiser John Hurt said, 'Wacky behaviour may seem like a lot of fun, but it usually isn't. It's usually the sign of a very distressed person looking for something they can't find.'

THEY'RE TRYING TO DISTRACT THEMSELVES FROM SOME PART OF THEIR LIVES OR THEMSELVES THAT THEY CAN'T COPE WITH

It's hard being 13

It's also hard being 2. And 70. And 17. There are inherent problems that go with all ages and stages. Some of us have it a bit easier than others, and some situations add to the stress.

Let's take 13 as an example. You might remember this[5] as a time of mental turmoil. Teenagers brains go through huge changes, and their emotions are being pulled all ways (more of this in some of the next few Rules). It's hard to assess risk, and hard to communicate. Those aren't moods, by the way, they're facts.

Seventy, and thereabouts. Almost anyone who reaches this age without a partner (and actually plenty who reach it with a partner) is likely to be lonely, unless they've managed to find a way to stave it off. We're all designed to lavish more love on the generation after us than the one before, so by the time you get to the top, you're quite possibly no one's most important person. Maybe not even close. And even the fittest 70-year-old has all sorts of aches and pains and trouble sleeping.

Or let's go back to 2. Toddlers have just started to realise they're not an extension of their parents but a person in their own right. This is baffling so they need to explore and experiment and find out how everything works. Only whenever they try, a big person comes along and tells them to stop.

Fifty or so. A lot of people this age are facing up to their kids leaving home. That's terrifying. Not only will you miss them, but what are you for now? You have to start afresh, but without the energy or time you had when you were 20.

And why am I telling you this? I find that if you ignore the context, it's much harder to understand why people behave as they do. You have to stand back and take a look at the bigger picture. There

---

[5] I'm assuming you've already been 13 by the time you read this. If not, please don't be put off.

are things we take in our stride at 20, and then somehow struggle with at 40, which is not the way round you'd expect. But it's all about what's going on in the rest of your life.

For example – if you haven't already discovered this for yourself – it's a lot harder to work long hours when you're middle-aged than it was 20 years before. Maybe that's why your parents don't agree that starting a business is the 'obvious' way to keep busy when you leave home. They also know more than they used to about what can go wrong, and it's a bigger risk now they're homeowners with the mortgage just about paid off.

Equally, your 17-year-old doesn't have your perspective on life and can't see that going away to university somewhere distant might be scary but it's fine once you've settled in. They just see that it's scary.

So take a step back and consider all the other stresses, fears, anxieties, pressures and worries in other people's lives before you judge them, or unwittingly add to the load.

IF YOU IGNORE THE CONTEXT, IT'S MUCH HARDER TO UNDERSTAND WHY PEOPLE BEHAVE AS THEY DO

RULE 24

They'll shout if you do

A friend once asked me, 'How do you get your kids to understand "do as I say, not as I do"?' The answer is very simple. It can't be done. Kids are programmed to learn by example, and there's no way round it.

What it boils down to is this: if you expect your kids to do it, why on earth are you not doing it yourself? Whether it's being tidy, saying please, eating vegetables, putting phones away at mealtimes[6], being ill without moaning constantly, putting the front door key down where you can find it again... if you can't do it, what makes you think a child will be able to? Either set the example you want them to follow, or live with them behaving like you.

Of course it's irritating when the kids leave toast crumbs in the butter on the one day you managed not to, but there are worse behaviours they can copy. Having teenagers at the moment (indeed, I can't really remember a time when I didn't...) I have lots of friends with teenagers. And it's very striking that those who complain their kids shout at them are – no prizes here – the ones who shout at their kids.

God knows it can be tempting to shout at them. And over the years it becomes a habit. They'll shout back, obviously, and by the time they become teenagers they'll be better at it than we are. They just have more energy. But by then it's far too late for you to turn into a not-shouty person. It's tough, it really is, especially if you were raised by shouty parents. But the only way to stop passing it down the generations is for you to learn to stop.

There are other examples too, mind you. Plenty of them. Parents who have always driven too fast while texting/after drinking, who discover their kids think it's normal and acceptable, and do it too.

---

[6] Ha! Did I get you with that one? If not, you're in a very small minority, and well done.

Parents who are openly picky about food, but who moan that their kids are fussy eaters. Or parents who bang on for years about their weight and which diet they're going on next, who find their teenage kids developing worrying eating habits.

Look, none of us is perfect. I get this wrong too, even after decades of practice. How could I have been so stupid as to think my kids wouldn't copy my habit of talking over other people? No, actually, I can answer that. I didn't think it. I didn't think anything about it at all. Had I *actually thought*, I would have realised how stupid it was. Maybe I'd even have stopped doing it.

And there's the biggest challenge. You have to recognise your shortcomings, and be able to control them. Otherwise you're wasting your breath telling the kids to stop.

> # IF YOU EXPECT YOUR KIDS TO DO IT, WHY ON EARTH ARE YOU NOT DOING IT YOURSELF?

Responsibility creates independence

If we want to raise well-adjusted kids, there are certain principles we have to grasp about how children work. We can't get the job right if we don't understand what's happening. It's our job to make sure that by the time our child turns 18 they are capable of living independently. Even if circumstances mean that they go on living with us for a while, they should still be doing it in an independent fashion. You know, doing their own laundry, handling their own finances, coping emotionally when we're away on holiday or wherever.

So what makes someone independent? Well, it's about taking responsibility for yourself. It's about not feeling you have to dump your worries, your decisions, your laundry on someone else in order to be able to cope with normal life. So the way to create an independent adult is to give them responsibility. Not all in a rush when they're 17. Gradually over time from a very early age.

Even a toddler can choose their own clothes for the day (you can control the options). A 6-year-old can decide for themselves whether they'll need a coat when they go outside. Yes, they can. Explain to them that it's going to be their decision from now on, and when they're cold at the end of the day they'll understand why they might want a coat tomorrow. You can remind them to think about it ('Do you reckon you might need a coat today?') but it's their choice. If you tell them when to wear a coat, how will they learn?

By the time they reach their teens, you can start helping them to manage money – for example, instead of buying their clothes for them, give them an allowance to buy their own. They'll need to learn that if they spend it all on party clothes, they'll have nothing to wear the rest of the time. If they make this mistake, don't give them more clothes. Make them live with the consequences until their next allowance. Otherwise you'll be taking their responsibility away from them. So what will they have learnt?

By the time your teenager gets to the top years of school, they should be setting their own work timetable. It should be their responsibility how much homework they do and when. That can be pretty scary as a parent because it means they might not get the grades they could if you'd set the pace. But these are is *their* grades we're talking about, not yours. Theirs to make, theirs to miss. And live with the consequences. Or what have they learnt?

If, like me, you have several children, this is easier to achieve, simply because you can't keep making decisions for so many other people. There aren't enough hours in the day. It's toughest if you have only one or two children. I have a friend with one child who once said to me, 'He needs to take a year off before university. He isn't ready to live away from home yet.' I made vaguely polite noises of sympathy but inside I was shouting, 'Why not? What have you been doing for the last eighteen years? This was your *only* job!'

> # IT'S ABOUT NOT FEELING YOU HAVE TO DUMP YOUR WORRIES, YOUR DECISIONS, YOUR LAUNDRY ON SOMEONE ELSE

Teenagers hate you because they love you

One of my teenagers voluntarily came over to me for a hug the other day. As I raised my arms to hug him back he said, 'Get off! Don't touch me.' And there you have the essence of teenagehood in a nutshell.

At the heart of being a teenager is a dilemma. On the one hand, they have an instinctive drive to be independent, and on the other hand they're terrified of being grown-up and want you to go on looking after them forever.

This is why they can simultaneously want you to hug them, and not to touch them – half of them is longing for reassurance while the other half knows it's time to go it alone. It's almost impossible to steer a steady course through the middle of these two conflicting drives, so they spend a lot of time flipping between the extremes. Some of them can literally fluctuate within moments between telling you they hate you and sobbing on your shoulder in a way they'd never do if they didn't love you. They hate you precisely because they feel their love for you is pulling them back from the growing up they know they have to do.

Here's something I've observed over the years – with only occasional exceptions where other significant forces are in play: the kids who find being a teenager the hardest are the ones who have a really strong independent streak, but are also very insecure. They're flip-flopping between the two widest extremes. Those who find it broadly easiest are the ones who are very secure and confident, and not in any particular rush to become independent.

Of course, most teenagers fall somewhere between these two extremes, but you can see the idea. So if you're a parent, you need to help your child to become independent – following the last two Rules among other things – as much as you can. The sooner they acquire adult skills and habits, the sooner they'll recognise that being a grown-up isn't so scary after all, and they can do it. That's why you have to stop making their decisions for them, picking up after them, supplying them with clothes and money, organising their time. Not all at once – you need to step away slowly. Starting from when they're about two.

Becoming a grown-up is emotionally hard work, however much you've been practising since you were young, which is why kids occasionally and suddenly need a hug. And after that they'll rant or grump at you a bit more and let you know why you're nothing but an encumbrance in their lives (even though, within another five minutes, they'll be asking you for money, a lift, help with their homework, money, help finding their socks, permission to use the house for a party, and money).

Once they feel they've made it to adulthood successfully, then you can go back to mutually agreed hugging. But first you'll probably have to go through a couple of years when you've no idea from one moment to the next what mood they're in. That's because they've no idea either.

BECOMING A GROWN-UP IS EMOTIONALLY HARD WORK

RULE 27

Talking is what matters

Right. So teenagers are torn between the scariness of growing up, and the temptations of staying dependent on you. But they know that they have no choice and the growing up has to happen. So – and listen closely because this bit is important – the only way they can cope with growing up is if they're absolutely certain that you'll still be there if they need you. That the staying dependent choice isn't really being taken away from them – it's just them who are moving away from it. The safety net is always there.

Suppose your 3-year-old comes to you sobbing because their Lego toy has fallen apart. What do you do? You sympathise, explain how to stop it breaking (don't drop it, or stamp on it, or leave it for the dog to play with), and help them put it back together. That means they can go on to build themselves bigger and better things, knowing that if it goes horribly wrong you'll help them sort it out.

Now fast forward 10 or 12 years. And let me give you an example involving some kids I know. Three of them secretly decided that they wanted to know what it was like to smoke cannabis. The grown-ups had all told them it was BAD, but they were old enough to be aware that lots of people did it with no obvious ill effects. So they weren't sure the grown-ups were telling them the truth, and they decided to find out for themselves. They managed to get hold of a small amount of the stuff, and tried smoking it one evening. As it happens, it made them cough horribly and they resolved never to touch it again.

But, being teenagers, they couldn't resist bragging a bit at school. And someone told a teacher. Who told the parents. Now imagine you're one of those parents. What are you going to do? (Remembering the bit that I told you earlier was very important.) I can tell you how the three parents reacted, if that helps. They all dealt with it differently:

- One parent shouted at their child about what a disappointment she was and how disgusted they were. She eventually took herself off to bed, where she was woken at 6am the following morning to be told again what a disappointment she was.

- One parent was angry with their child and banned them from visiting their friends' houses.

- One parent talked to their child about the pros and cons of drugs, and discussed the incident with them. They didn't get angry and didn't impose any sanctions.

Now, which of these teenagers knew that their parents were there for them just like they used to be? That growing up is scary, and we all make mistakes, but their parents were still there to help? And, most importantly of all, which one of these kids is going to tell their parents next time they're in trouble and can't fix it on their own?

Once they reach mid-teens, you should have instilled in them about as much sense as you'll get the chance to. They need to do this growing up stuff by themselves, mistakes and all. And the *only* thing you can usefully do is make sure they'll talk to you when it goes wrong.

> # THEY NEED TO DO THIS GROWING UP STUFF BY THEMSELVES, MISTAKES AND ALL

Listening is what matters

Yes, I know I just said that talking was what mattered, and now I'm saying listening is what matters. Don't get picky with me, smart-arse! Haven't you been listening yourself, anyway? We've just established that being a teenager is a mass of apparent contradictions which do actually make sense deep down. So now I'm joining in. Talking *and* listening are both what matter. And not only with teenagers, as I hope you'll realise. This Rule goes for anyone.

You know, sometimes parents can be just like teenagers – they think they know everything. They've been teenagers themselves, they've learnt stuff since then that their kids don't understand, they can see the bigger picture – yep, they're confident they can tell their kids where they're going wrong and what they need to do to get on in life.

But that's not true. Your child isn't the same as you, or the same as anyone else. They're growing up in a very different world from the one you were raised in. They have their own unique plans and dreams and strengths and fears and hopes. And you have no idea whatever where they're coming from or where they're going, apart from the few snippets of information you can glean from them. If you're listening.

Your only hope of understanding your child is to listen to what they're telling you. That doesn't mean pausing until they've finished talking and then carrying on regardless. It means properly paying attention, and taking it on board. If their feelings don't make sense to you, it doesn't mean your child has no sense, it means you haven't managed to understand them yet. So try harder.

If your child can see that you're actually making a real effort to see things from their perspective, they'll help you. Maybe not every time – they have busy lives, and lie-ins to find time for, and days when expressing themselves doesn't come easy – but they want you to see things their way, so by and large they'll explain themselves. But only if you listen and adapt to what they're saying. If they know that whatever they say you'll go back to your usual theme – banging on about how they need to work harder, or how the world doesn't owe them a living, or how they're too young to understand, or how manners cost nothing, or how early bedtimes are important – why should they bother even trying to explain themselves? Why make the effort if it's going to fall on deaf ears?

So do your very best to imagine what it must be like to be them, rather than what you would do if you were in their position yourself. Ask questions that show you really want to get your head round their perspective. You don't have to agree with everything they say, or abandon all the rules they don't care for. But understand why they struggle with them. They might have a point, you know. Maybe there's room for compromise, or keeping to one rule but allowing them a different freedom in exchange.

In the last Rule, the third parent didn't play the heavy-handed enforcer because they listened. They understood how a teenager might want to explore the world for themselves and not just take the adult view at face value. And they realised – because they listened – that their child had learnt for themselves that they didn't want to repeat the experience. That's how they knew they didn't need to berate or punish their child.

> # LISTEN TO WHAT THEY'RE TELLING YOU. THAT DOESN'T MEAN PAUSING UNTIL THEY'VE FINISHED TALKING

No one likes saying sorry[7]

I had two friends who fell out with each other. It wasn't a big deal really, but it took them months to make up afterwards. For one simple reason: they each insisted that the other one apologised. And neither wanted to lose face, especially when they felt it was the other one who should apologise. Over time they were civil when they couldn't avoid seeing each other, and in the end things got back to normal – without the falling-out ever really being discussed – because actually they liked each other and wanted to be friends. They just wasted several months over the 'sorry' thing.

Look, it really doesn't matter whether the other person says sorry when there's a falling-out. What matters is how they feel and how they act, not the words they say. Words are cheap. Personally I don't like the practice of making kids say sorry to each other when they behave badly. It's meaningless. We should be helping our kids to *feel* sorry, not simply mouth the word.

One of my kids was once berated by a teacher for not saying sorry as if he meant it. He told me, 'It wasn't true! I apologised as sincerely as I would have done if I'd actually *been* sorry.' See? The teacher achieved nothing. Whereas if she'd sat my child down and explained why his behaviour had upset his friend, he might have felt genuinely repentant.

The word sorry isn't the important bit. When you fall out with a colleague, a friend, a partner, let them save face by making their regret clear without being forced to go through the process of saying 'sorry', which can feel humiliating. Their genuine concern

---

[7] Unless they're English, of course, in which case they'll revel in saying sorry, but only for things that don't matter, like bumping into strangers (or being bumped into by strangers, which most English people will also apologise for). For everything that actually matters, however, this Rule applies to the English as much as everyone else.

for you and desire to make things OK is surely more important than that one silly word.

If someone makes an effort to smile and say good morning when you come in to work, that's their way of letting you know that they don't like the unpleasantness between you. Maybe – at some point – you might need a friendly chat about what went wrong, why it upset you, how to avoid it happening again. But the friendly smile is there to let you know the other person is OK with that.

You know, maybe they feel that *they* were the injured party, and that your behaviour warranted an apology. But the smile lets you know they're prepared to overlook it. So maybe that smile says they're (genuinely) sorry, *and* they forgive you too. All you have to do is smile back, by way of apology and forgiveness yourself, and the whole thing is practically sorted with no need for anyone to say sorry. Alternatively you could both grunt 'sorry' at each other like naughty children and not actually feel sorry at all. Now which makes most sense to you?

Having said all that – if you recognise that you're out of order in any way, and you're big enough, you could just say sorry anyway.

> # WHAT MATTERS IS HOW THEY FEEL AND HOW THEY ACT, NOT THE WORDS THEY SAY

The world is full of rebels

A friend of mine at school was amazingly resilient when being shouted at by teachers. I have to say I didn't mind being told off as much as some, but this guy was so unaffected even I was impressed. I was at school with him for years and I remember hearing once that he'd been on the receiving end of a serious telling-off from a teacher in a lesson I wasn't in. So I asked him what it was all about. He told me he had no idea. I pointed out that he must have had some idea what the teacher was so angry about, if only from the words the teacher was shouting. He looked surprised and said, as though it should have been obvious, 'I have no idea what he was saying. I wasn't listening.' I wasn't expecting this, so I asked him to explain himself. His reply was this: 'I never listen when teachers are cross with me. If I listened, this little voice inside my head would be telling me to do exactly what the teacher is telling me *not* to. And that's never going to be a good idea. So I just don't listen. I can't do the opposite if I don't know what it is.'

I was delighted with the brilliance of his response, and on occasion I have used various adaptations of it since then. Because I'm like him – I also have a little voice in my head telling me to rebel against whatever I'm being told to do. Lots of us do, although I suspect we're still a minority. Some people, on being told what to do, will appreciate the guidance, or accept the directive, or follow the instruction. Others find it more difficult to do as we're told.

You need to identify the people around you who are secret rebels, because telling them what to do can backfire. If you're their boss, you might encounter quiet resistance, or a determination to do things their way and not yours. If you're their parent or partner or friend, things can get a lot shoutier than that.

You have two options here. The first is to adopt reverse psychology – this works especially well with kids. Tell them not to do the thing you actually want them to do, and you should both be happy. Just don't let them know afterwards that you manipulated them or they will be furious (and the ploy will never work again).

The other way to handle a secret rebel is to avoid giving them any more instruction than necessary. Indeed, if you can, let them know that you're not trying to control or direct them in any way. Set the parameters you have to, and leave them to get on with it in their own style: 'The research needs to be completed by Friday week, and I particularly want to know where the competition are on this. I'm sure you can work out the best way to go about it, so just ask if you need anything from me.'

The rule with rebels is the less you give them to kick against, the less they'll rebel. More than that indeed – they'll appreciate being allowed to do things their own way.

TELLING THEM WHAT TO DO CAN BACKFIRE

Some weirdos are great people

We're all pretty conventional as a social species. We like what we know – of course we do. We feel safe with what we know. And that applies to people as much as situations. You can tell so much about someone from the way they dress, speak, behave, wear their hair. When you meet someone new, you can pretty much pigeon-hole them straight away. You can see what type they are.

So it's quite disconcerting when you meet someone you can't categorise. Someone who stands out as being different. That doesn't feel safe at all. In many ways, the easiest thing is to avoid them if at all possible. Especially if they come across as someone who not only looks odd, but also seems to follow different social rules – you know, they don't get the unspoken stuff about where to stand or when to speak or how to address people.

What's interesting is that it's all to do with fitting in with other people. If you go to places where everyone is like this, suddenly it becomes acceptable, the norm, expected. And then the weirdos aren't weirdos at all. I used to live in Glastonbury, in southwest England, which is where the hippies hang out. A friend of mine once described them as people who 'like rainbow colours, don't brush their hair, and wear all their clothes at once'. They also talk a lot about chakras and healing crystals and how there's no such thing as coincidence[8] because everything is 'meant to be'. If you meet one of these people in Glastonbury – which you will – you don't even notice because they blend into the crowd. But if the same person turned up at an office furniture sales conference, you'd definitely mark them down as a weirdo. Same person, different scenario.

---

[8] Which if you think about it would be the most extraordinary coincidence.

Of course, if you were a hippy working in office furniture, you'd probably save the rainbow clothes for your days off. But all these people are doing is being themselves in every situation, instead of trying to blend with the crowd. Whether it's a deliberate choice or an inability to recognise the effect they have doesn't really matter – the point is that they're simply being themselves. Which is rather refreshing actually, don't you think?

Once you step out of your safety zone and speak to these people, they can be among the most interesting and inspiring people to know. Obviously – as with all people – a few of them might be tedious or not very nice, but it's no more likely than with any other group. Sometimes they have intriguing backstories which shed light on why they appear as they do. Sometimes they're quite brilliant at their jobs. Sometimes they're exceptionally kind. Just like all of us.

If you play it safe and give the weirdos of this world a wide berth, you deprive yourself of the chance to know someone who might be a real positive in your life, in a small way or even a big way. And you miss the chance to learn that stepping out of your safety zone will enrich your life. So what's to lose? Stop avoiding people you can't quite get the measure of, and go and find out first-hand what they're really like and how they tick.

> ## ALL THESE PEOPLE ARE DOING IS BEING THEMSELVES IN EVERY SITUATION

HELPING
PEOPLE

It's miserable when the people you care about are in trouble – for you as well as for them. You just want to do everything you can to make it better for them. But what can you do?

From the frustration of working with a colleague who seems unable to co-operate, through to the heartbreak of watching your child or close family struggling with life, you just want to be of practical use. Part of the solution.

Even without considering what the problem is, there are certain Rules that always apply. Basic tenets that I've spent a lifetime observing in practice – and I have come to realise that any help will be better if you follow these Rules. They are all about creating an interaction that gives the other person freedom to find their own way through their troubles, strengthened by knowing that you're on their side. You might well notice how these Rules would help when other people are trying to help you too.

RULE 32

Put your oxygen mask on first

It's important to help people who need it, for two overriding reasons in particular. The first is the glaringly obvious one that – well, they need it. And the other is that helping other people makes you feel good about yourself.[9] So ideally you should help out wherever help is wanted, and everyone's a winner.

Hang on a minute though. This works fine if you're carrying someone's heavy shopping, or giving a stranger directions, or cooking dinner for your exhausted partner, or photocopying a colleague's report, or saving a bird with an injured wing. But suppose your friend is struggling with grief, or one of your family has been diagnosed bipolar, or your colleague's marriage is falling apart?

Any one – or more – of these scenarios might seem pretty straightforward to you, and indeed you might be perfectly equipped to help. Then again, your colleague might have turned to you because you know what it's like after your own marriage fell apart a few months ago. Maybe you could bring great insight as a result. But can you cope with picking over someone else's marriage when your own experience is so raw? Might it re-open recent wounds and be simply too painful for you?

People often ask for support from someone who has been through a similar experience. It makes logical sense, and frequently we're more than happy to pass on anything we've learnt. We feel we can make a real difference, and often we can. But look at the other examples I just gave. Your friend who is grieving, the bipolar relative – you could be the best person to turn to from their perspective, but from your own viewpoint it might seem like the worst idea ever.

---

[9] See Rule 34 of *The Rules to Break* if you want more on this.

And you have to protect yourself, you really do. Because if you are overcome by emotion, you'll be very little use to the other person. They need you to be strong, and they also need to be able to focus on themselves for a bit, and not have to worry about how they're affecting you.

Actually, in some cases, it's not so much your own past that is the problem but the person themselves. For example, spending a lot of time around someone struggling with alcohol dependency or severe depression or other mental health issues might bring you right down. Up to a point it goes with the territory when you help someone else, but there's a line — only you know where it is — beyond which it can damage you significantly.

You have to make sure you are in a fit state to help, and to get on with the rest of your life. If necessary, you might even have to make your apologies and explain this is just too raw right now. You may still be able to help in other more practical ways rather than listening. However, perhaps just limiting the time you spend together or controlling the circumstances might do it for you. If your life is deeply interwoven with the other person, you'll need to find ways to get the oxygen you need without abandoning them — long walks, seeing friends, joining a local amdram society or sports club. The important thing is that you recognise the importance of being emotionally capable yourself in order to be of real help.

> # IF YOU ARE OVERCOME BY EMOTION, YOU'LL BE VERY LITTLE USE TO THE OTHER PERSON

RULE 33

Get in the swamp

Recognise this? Your partner, or someone close to you, tells you they're upset about something. You listen and then start making suggestions as to how to solve their problem. And instead of being grateful, they get more upset and now it seems to be partly your fault but you've no idea why...

Trust me, it's not only you this happens to. In fact you have probably experienced this from the other side yourself – you feel upset and your partner (or whoever) keeps offering solutions to your problem and it really winds you up. You don't know why – clearly they're trying to help – but it just isn't helping and you're starting to regret mentioning it to them at all.

Whichever one of you is upset in this scenario is getting frustrated by offers of help from the other one, even though the upset person appears to be asking for help. So what's going on?

The fact is, there's something else you need first before you need solutions. If the person who is upset doesn't recognise this need (and most of us don't), they won't ask for it. But they'll still feel frustrated they're not getting it, even though they're not sure what it is they're not getting. Right, so what does your partner or friend want you to do even before you try to help them? Answering this question is the key to making these conversations go smoothly and leaving everyone feeling happier.

They want your permission to feel what they're feeling, that's what. I know it makes very little sense a lot of the time, but feelings aren't rational. The thing is, if you go straight into offering solutions, it appears to imply that the other person shouldn't be upset or angry or worried because look, there's a solution. But the other person *does* feel upset or angry or worried, and now on top of their problems you seem to be telling them their feelings are invalid. That's the hidden subtext (yes, I know that isn't what you actually meant at all).

The best analogy I know for this is to imagine the other person is stuck in a swamp and you're standing on the edge. The way to help is not to throw them a rope, but to get into the swamp with them and agree how swampy it is. Then you can hold hands and get out of the swamp together instead of you pulling them out from the edge.

So before you even think about saying, 'How about...' or 'Why don't you...' or 'What if you were to...', you need to graciously confer your permission to be upset. Just say something like, 'I'm not surprised you're angry', or 'I'd be really upset in your position', or 'No wonder you're worried'.

Once they know they're allowed to feel as they do, they can relax and think about solutions for themselves. Which goes to show that often they didn't actually need help at all, they just wanted their feelings validated. I have no idea why so few people recognise this need in themselves, but there it is. So you'll have to do it for them (and for yourself when the roles are reversed).

THERE'S SOMETHING ELSE YOU NEED FIRST BEFORE YOU NEED SOLUTIONS

It's OK just to feel

Following on from the last Rule, many people have a sense that somehow feelings don't count unless there's a good rational 'reason' for them. I'm not sure where this comes from, and it seems to be more prevalent in some cultures than others. But it does help the last Rule to make sense.

You and I – here on this page – we know perfectly well that feelings are what they are and we don't have to be able to justify them. But out there in the real world almost everyone – you and me included – can sometimes feel embarrassed or ashamed or shy or insecure about admitting how we feel. As though we have made a rational choice to feel that way and are therefore responsible for it. Yes, you can sometimes choose how to feel, but it takes practice; it usually takes time to change a particular response, and it doesn't always work anyway. The stronger the feeling, the harder it gets.

When you're dealing with other people, it can sometimes be difficult to help them because they don't tell you what they're feeling. Often the reason for this is precisely what I'm talking about – they feel embarrassed to tell you how they feel in case you think they're being silly or stupid or unreasonable or illogical or over-reacting. In fact, the sillier someone says they feel they are being, the more genuine the hurt usually is – and the more you can probably help. So you need to let them know that you won't judge their emotions.

As with the last Rule, you can let the other person know that you expect them to respond emotionally (i.e. you're telling them that's normal and nothing to be ashamed of). Just ask them, depending on the situation, 'Are you angry?' or 'Do you feel hurt?' or whatever. The fact that you've asked tells them it's OK to say yes, they do. You're clearly assuming this is a reasonable response.

This can be the spur that enables them to open up to you and let you help them. Once they know they won't be judged, they can speak freely. And talking about things with someone who is prepared to listen without judgement is, for many people, the road to resolving them – whether it's about finding solutions, or simply about getting it off their chest.

By the way, you also need to guard against any remarks that give the opposite impression. If someone tells you they're worried and you reply, 'Don't be', you might think you're reassuring them, but what they hear is that their feeling is somehow not permitted. When you tell someone 'Don't cry', they hear, 'This doesn't warrant crying'. When people are in any kind of emotional state, they feel shakier. So they could easily interpret your 'Don't worry' as dismissive rather than reassuring.

Other people's emotions can be like small nervous kittens. They're not going to come out from under the sofa unless you coax them carefully and let them know you're on their side.

> # OTHER PEOPLE'S EMOTIONS CAN BE LIKE SMALL NERVOUS KITTENS

Listen, don't solve

Sometimes people want practical help – a lift because their car has broken down, a brief loan of your phone because theirs is out of charge, advice on putting together a CV because you've got way more experience than them. That's fine, because it's a pragmatic need that you can supply. Once you've done what they ask, the problem is resolved. Well done, and give yourself a pat on the back for being a good citizen, neighbour, friend.

However, once emotions come into play, it's a different matter. You can't fix other people's emotions and that's not your job. When someone is upset or angry or worried or scared, they need to sort out the feelings inside their head, and you can't do that for them. They're talking to you about it because they want a sounding board, not a solution.

It took my wife years to get this through to me, because my natural instinct when someone brings me a problem is to try to solve it. As she pointed out, in clear and unambiguous terms, that can be quite patronising. The implication is that she can't solve her own problems for herself. If she wants to borrow a screwdriver, or ask for a lift, she'll say so (she points out). She doesn't – I gather – appreciate help she never asked for.

I have to admit, it turns out my wife is not alone here. After hearing many other people moaning about their partners not listening to them, I have come to realise that she's quite right. And the clue is right there – 'not listening' to them. You see, the moment you start trying to fix someone's problem for them, you stop listening to it.

They have come to you to get things off their chest, perhaps to validate their feelings (as in the last couple of Rules), and maybe to help them find clarity by talking things over. Unless they actually asked you to help, they probably don't want you to. They just want you to listen. So sit on your hands, bite your tongue, repress your urge to *do* something. You are already doing something. You're listening. That's a thing, and you're doing it. It's enough.

The other person may reach a point, if you do your listening well, where they're ready to start looking for solutions. Or not, because they might already know what they're going to do, and they just wanted to talk it through first. If you sense that maybe they will actually welcome suggestions from you, you can always check. 'Are you looking for ideas, or do you just need to get it off your chest?' Indeed my recommendation, especially in relationships, is always to ask this question. That would be my wife's advice too. Apparently.

> # REPRESS YOUR URGE TO *DO* SOMETHING. YOU ARE ALREADY DOING SOMETHING. YOU'RE LISTENING

Know your limitations

In one sense helping other people is all about them, but of course it's about you as well. You're going to be doing the helping: covering for them at work while they're away, cooking freezer meals for them while they're laid up with a bad back, taking their kids to school for a couple of weeks, coming to the hospital with them for their test results.

I've already talked about putting your oxygen mask on first, to protect yourself from emotional fallout. But even when the help is more practical, you have to be honest about what is attainable. If you offer to cover for a colleague at work and then find you can't cope, how will that help them? Suppose you promise to go to the hospital with them and then find at the last minute you have a work commitment you can't get out of?

In both these examples, it would have been more helpful to say no right from the start, rather than to make the right noises but not follow through. The trouble is, for many of us, we so want to help that we make over-ambitious offers of support. 'Yes, I can do that.' 'Just leave it with me.' 'Don't give it another thought.' 'I've got it.' 'No need to worry.'

Actually, perhaps you knew deep down that if the hospital appointment coincided with your client's visit, you wouldn't make it. You figured it was so unlikely, why worry about it. But you've made it much harder for your friend to find someone else at such short notice. You didn't have to say no – you could just have warned them of the risk and let them decide whether to chance it or to ask someone else.

I know you're coming from the right place, you really want to help, but understand that letting someone down later because you weren't honest with yourself can be far worse than saying no right from the off.

I once offered to help out with school runs for a friend who had a bad back. I thought it would be for a week or two (I'm always over-optimistic – she never actually specified a time limit). Six weeks later I was still doing it. Trouble was, it was a different school from my kids and added another 15 minutes every morning and afternoon. That meant less time at my desk each day, and losing well over two hours' work a week. After six weeks, I was really regretting my offer. If I'd thought about it, I'd have realised this was beyond what I could spare. I could have said I'd do it for a couple of weeks, or that I'd do mornings if she could get someone else to do afternoons...I could have said a lot of things, but instead I just said yes. At least in this case it was me and not her who suffered for my stupidity. And I learnt a very useful lesson (which I'm now passing on to you).

So know your limitations, and don't offer more than you're confident you can deliver. Otherwise, either one or both of you will be sorry.

> # DON'T OFFER MORE THAN YOU'RE CONFIDENT YOU CAN DELIVER

It's not a competition

A friend of mine sadly lost her husband a few years ago. One of the things that she found most surprising was the number of people who felt it necessary to compare their situation with hers. One of her friends going through a divorce told her, 'At least you knew he wasn't coming back.' Another friend explained how dreadful her father's death had been for her mother because they'd been together nearly 50 years – said in a way that clearly meant my friend's loss (after only 20 years together) wasn't nearly so bad.

The fact is that telling someone their situation isn't as bad as they think is never going to go down well. They know how bad it is (and you don't). If someone has recently been bereaved, divorced, made redundant, become seriously ill, the likelihood of them suddenly feeling better about it because you've pointed out how much worse off you are is zilch.

My friend can list all the people who upset her in this way, and is wary of their friendship now as a result. However, she doesn't have a list, of any sort, of people who talked through their difficulties without comparing them to hers. Because that isn't a problem. Life goes on and even people going through traumatic times recognise that everyone else has their challenges and it's good to talk. In fact, supporting other people through their own difficulties can be a welcome distraction from their own.

Of course, you need some sensitivity. Collapsing in tears all over someone who has recently been diagnosed with a serious illness because your pet hamster is unwell might be a little thoughtless. Perhaps find a different shoulder to cry on for that. And sometimes it's considerate to say, 'I realise my problems are nothing like as bad as what you're going through,' especially if your two situations have some similarity. It just reassures them you haven't underestimated their grief or suffering. But beyond that, just keep things separate and, above all, don't compete.

It's human nature to compare notes, because it shows empathy. Your friend says, 'I'm really worried I might lose my job,' and you reply, 'I know what that's like – my company is making redundancies too.' That's good – it shows you understand. But if you want people to value you as a friend, you have to make sure you don't cross the line into trying to one-up them – 'You think you have problems? They're laying people off all over the place in my company right now, and it's really hard to find another job in my line of work.' See? You've gone from making your friend feel he's not alone, to making him feel he has no right to complain.

The key here is that if your friend or colleague is having a moan and getting things off their chest, or if they're going through a particularly tough time, the focus is on them and how they feel, not on you. You can have your moan next time.

> THE LIKELIHOOD OF THEM
> SUDDENLY FEELING BETTER
> BECAUSE YOU'VE POINTED OUT
> HOW MUCH WORSE OFF YOU
> ARE IS ZILCH

Never give advice

Yes, ironically I am advising you – strongly – never to give advice. But this is different because you chose to buy this book, read it, consider its contents. And I'll never know, if you don't tell me, whether you've followed my advice or not.

When it comes to friends, colleagues, family, or anyone else you know personally, however, just don't give advice. Again, I'm not talking practical stuff (do these shoes go with my outfit, what can I cook for dinner tonight, what font would you use for this report?) You can answer those safely – if you know the answer. It's the stuff with an emotional angle you want to keep out of. Listen, sympathise, support, but don't advise.

Yes, even if they ask you: Should I just tell my boss where to get off? Is it time to move my mum into a nursing home? I'm thinking of applying for a new job – what do you think?

Why? Because you have no idea what will work for someone else. Not necessarily the same things that work for you, I can tell you that. So how can you be sure it's even the right advice? Also, because people need to arrive at their own decisions in order to feel committed to them and to have the confidence to see them through. So you've deprived them of a vital stage in the decision-making process if you tell them what to do. And because if you answer their question, you've cut to the end point, but actually it's essential for them to go through the process of thinking it through, weighing up the options, considering all the arguments.

And hey, what if you're wrong? What if they tell the boss how they really feel, and get taken off the team? Or put their mum in a nursing home and feel guilty about it for evermore? Maybe you weren't even wrong. Maybe your advice really was the best thing on paper, but they might still regret it, and/or blame it on you.

Set against all this the arguments in favour of giving advice: hmmm... Can't think of any of those, unless perhaps it makes you feel good. But we're trying to help other people here, so arguments about what it does for you aren't relevant. What's the case from their perspective of being given advice? Even if they think they want it, how can it really be in their best interest?

Take into account that you're simply wasting your breath giving advice that won't be heeded. Suppose your friend is with an abusive partner. Do you think they don't know they should leave? You telling them so will just make them feel more useless when they can't do it. It won't help them leave – you'll just be one more person trying to control them. They need support, not instructions they can't follow.

So what are you supposed to do, especially when someone asks directly for advice? The answer is to respond with questions, and help them find the right answer for themselves. How would you feel if...? Suppose that...? Keep thinking of options – without recommending them – and help them think through the ramifications and how they would feel in each case. Then you'll have really helped.

> # YOU HAVE NO IDEA WHAT WILL WORK FOR SOMEONE ELSE

Accept their decision

This sounds like an easy Rule to follow, and it often is. If your colleague decides to put up with the boss criticising them, or your friend plumps for having their mum come and live with them, or your brother hands in his notice and starts applying for jobs, why should you mind? It's their life, you did what you could to help them choose what to do (without giving them advice), and you reckon they'll be happier this way. Win/win all round, and you go and find someone else to help next.

Ah, but it's not really that simple, is it? Secretly, you were kind of hoping your colleague would tell the boss where to get off. Because if it works, you could get the benefit too. And if it all goes horribly wrong, well, you're not in the firing line. Now you'll have to put up with it too, or else risk a confrontation.

And what if your brother finds a job out of the area? Your parents rely on him so heavily, they'll be devastated if he's not there any-more, except for occasional visits.

And how about your friend? She might think it will work having her mum to live with her now she can't cope alone, but you know it won't. You've seen how someone in her mum's position can deteriorate rapidly. Six months or a year from now, your friend might not be able to leave her alone in the house. You know she's made the wrong decision. That's what comes of not giving advice – people make the wrong choices.

Or do they? Maybe your friend knows full well what might lie ahead. When you talked it over you didn't give her advice, but you did ask her, 'What if your mum deteriorates, how will that work?' Perhaps she's got a Plan B. Or perhaps she just knows she can't live with herself any other way so she'll cross that bridge when she comes to it. If she comes to it.

Sometimes, living with other people's decisions about their own lives can have an impact on you. Maybe, as with your colleague, their decision directly affects you. Your working relationship with the boss is tricky and your colleague has now put the ball in your court. It was still their decision to make though. Even if it has forced you into a decision of your own. You don't want anyone else telling you that you now have to confront the boss, so obviously it wouldn't be right to push your colleague into the decision. It's unfortunate that it puts you in a tricky position, but that's life.

Your friend's and brother's decisions don't change your life. But they still make you feel bad – for them, for other people. You might worry that if you'd given them better help and support, they'd have made a 'better' decision. So you could feel guilty as well as concerned.

Listen, for all the help you give, you can't interfere with someone else's decision, and you are not responsible for it. Any consequences that flow from it are strictly down to them. You need to understand this in order to avoid pointless feelings of guilt, worry or blame. Your role was only ever a supporting one – so long as you did that as well as you could, be satisfied.

> # OTHER PEOPLE'S DECISIONS ABOUT THEIR OWN LIVES CAN HAVE AN IMPACT ON YOU

Give them control

There's another reason why you have to accept other people's decisions if you're genuine about wanting to help them. It's important for everyone to feel in control of their own lives. If you start making their decisions for them – however well-meaning you are – you're taking away that control.

Yes, you might be right that they're heading towards disaster, but at least they're behind the wheel of their own car, and they have the option (whether they choose to take it or not) of turning down a side road, or slamming on the brakes. If you grab the steering wheel, they're going to feel even more terrified.

What's more, this is their car, and you don't know as well as they do how it drives. You might not have made allowances for the iffy clutch, or the indicators that don't work unless you waggle the lever.[10] So now they're even more anxious because no one knows their car – or their life – as well as they do.

A friend of mine who is a volunteer for the Samaritans tells me that sometimes people phone them who are suicidal because they feel they have no control over their lives. The Samaritans' policy is to listen and not give any advice – not even to tell them they mustn't take their own lives (whilst nevertheless trying to help them see an alternative for themselves). Apparently, this simple act of allowing them to make their own decision about suicide, permitting them control over their own life, can be the thing that helps them make the choice to continue living. A sense of control over our own lives is indeed that powerful.

So it's no surprise that for your friends, family and colleagues – who I hope are not suicidal – normal levels of happiness and well-being are reliant on the sense that they're in control of their

---

[10] I'm not encouraging you to drive a badly maintained vehicle. It's just a metaphor...

own lives. If they're always being told what to do, they'll feel anxious and unsafe. This can be a particular problem with teenagers who often feel they're being told what to do all the time. At such a vulnerable age, this can have serious consequences for their mental health.

There are few instances I can think of where taking control of other people's decisions does enough good to balance the harm inherent in taking away that control. I know you don't think you're controlling them, I know you think it's just good advice and they're free to ignore it, but if you give that advice too strongly to someone who is already anxious and vulnerable, it can feel to them as if you're making their decisions for them. And how it feels to them is the only bit that matters – your intentions are irrelevant.

> # YOU MIGHT BE RIGHT THAT THEY'RE HEADING TOWARDS DISASTER, BUT AT LEAST THEY'RE BEHIND THE WHEEL

Get them to think for themselves

I hope I didn't upset you in the last few Rules, suggesting you were making things worse for people when you were only trying to help. I realise you hate seeing people you care about upset, and you want to make things better. Quite right too.

So I have a suggestion. Why don't you help them to make better decisions for themselves? That way you won't be tempted to wade in, and they'll be more self-sufficient and happier. You'll still feel you've helped, so everyone's a winner. I can't promise they'll make the same decision you would, but then maybe what works for you wouldn't be right for them anyway. At least they'll have thought the whole thing through properly.

By the way, this approach works whether the other person asks you for advice directly, or whether they just come to you to talk over their problems. It's nice to know you have a one-size-fits-all response you can use. And it's just so simple. All you have to do is ask questions.

Yep, that's it. Easy, huh? Of course, they mustn't be leading questions which suggest their own answer. You want open questions – ones which require a full and proper answer, not just a yes or no response. You can start by asking the other person to tell you all about the problem. Even if you already know a lot of it, you're doing this for them not you. The process of describing it will help them to see it clearly, which in turn will help them find their way through.

Then you can start asking them more specific questions. Get them to explore all the options. Don't point them towards or away from anything, even if you're tempted. Got to do this properly or it won't work. And concentrate on their feelings because those are the bits that matter. It's not about solutions, so asking what will happen if... matters less than asking how they will feel if...

So explore all their options in terms of ifs and whethers: How would you feel if...? Suppose that...? Keep thinking of options – without recommending them – and get them to think clearly through all the possibilities before them. Let's say your friend is trying to decide whether to move in with their partner and they're really unsure. What if they do and the relationship breaks up? What if they do and things work well? What if one of them moves closer to the other so they can spend most of their time together? Help them think through the ramifications and how they would feel in each case.

I remember talking to someone who was absolutely torn about whether or not to risk turning a hobby into a commercial business. She was terrified it would all go wrong. Once she'd had a chance to think it through calmly however, she came to see that she could start in a small way and find out if she had a viable business idea with actually very little risk. It wasn't the huge worry she had supposed at all. She needn't scale up unless she could see it would work.

It's amazing how much difference thinking things through clearly can make. And sometimes it takes a friend like you to make it possible. No advice, no pressure. Just some really sensible, intelligent questions. Then you'll have really helped.

> # NO ADVICE, NO PRESSURE.
> # JUST SOME REALLY SENSIBLE,
> # INTELLIGENT QUESTIONS

RULE 42

Learn to be psychic

A friend of mine had an arrangement with her mother to look after her child some days when my friend was working. At the start of the new school year, my friend fixed a new rota with her mother, who said she was happy with it. But she kept phoning up to query it – 'What time did you say you needed me on Thursdays?' and so on. It became clear to my friend that her mum wasn't really happy at all, although she kept insisting it was all fine when my friend tried checking. The friend told me she just couldn't work out what the problem was, because her mum denied there was one. 'She wants me to be psychic,' my friend told me, 'but unfortunately I'm not'.

I was discussing this Rule with my editor a few weeks before writing this. She said, 'Yes, you have to know the right questions to ask because they're expecting you to, er...' At which point I unthinkingly added, '...fill in the blanks'. Thus expertly falling into my own trap.

We were right, though. The trick to coping with this is twofold. Firstly you have to realise that there's a subtext. Generally you'll know this from a vague sense that you're wading through treacle, that things aren't as straightforward underneath as they appear on the surface.

Then you have to get out of the treacle lake. The way to do that is to ask the right questions. Sometimes this is easy. It can be as simple as saying, 'There's something else bothering you, isn't there?' But other times either it doesn't feel right to ask, or it gets you nowhere because you can't get a clear answer. Indeed, sometimes the other person hasn't consciously acknowledged the subtext to themselves, in which case asking them straight out can't possibly work.

So you need to be clever about the questions you ask. Think about what the likely reasons are that might make the other person resist, and ask questions around that. They might not want to give you the real reason because they're embarrassed by it – they worry you'll dismiss it as petty or neurotic or silly – so you can help by letting them know that you wouldn't. 'I can understand it would be difficult for you if you felt . . .' might enable them to say, 'Well, yes, it is tricky'. Now you're making headway.

My friend surmised that the new times didn't really fit, but her mother was worried if she said so that my friend would find childcare elsewhere, leaving her mum less precious time with her grandchild. So she went back to her mum and asked some carefully chosen questions. Sure enough, her mother didn't want to say no but actually the new rota was clashing with other stuff in her life. Easily sorted, and of course my friend wanted to make things easy for her mother. She just had to do a lot of work herself to find out how.

> # YOU NEED TO BE CLEVER ABOUT THE QUESTIONS YOU ASK

RULE 43

Listen to what they don't say

The last Rule was about helping other people to solve a problem they don't acknowledge exists. This Rule is slightly different, and you might recognise the scenario: the other person is telling you that there is a problem but, however hard you try, you don't seem to be able to fix it.

It's extremely frustrating when this happens. Although it certainly isn't exclusive to relationships, it's most common between partners. In effect, the problem that is being raised is masking a deeper problem. So whatever you do to address the visible problem, you're only ever treating the symptom. You need to identify the underlying cause, and treat that.

This can be complicated by the fact that often the other person isn't consciously aware of what's going on either. They may genuinely believe that the symptom they're talking about is the whole problem. Let's give you an example. Your partner complains that you don't do enough housework. So, being helpful and wanting a smooth relationship, you either start doing more round the house, or you rationally talk through why this is difficult (your long hours at work, for example). Your partner agrees, but the problem doesn't go away – or maybe it shifts a bit. Next time perhaps you don't do your share of the washing up, or tidying the garden, or shopping.

As soon as you realise the problem isn't going away – either it just displaces slightly, or it keeps reappearing despite you thinking you've addressed it – that's the point when bells should go off in your head. Or lightbulbs, because this should be an 'Aha!' moment. It should trigger the realisation that the problem your partner is describing is not the real problem.

And generally, the issues in question are like an iceberg. The visible problem is being discussed, but below the waterline there's a much bigger problem lurking. That's your baby. That's the one you need to grapple with.

In the example I've just given, almost always the real issue is that your partner feels taken for granted. And just because you've started vacuuming around occasionally doesn't mean the problem's gone away. You addressed the problem they raised – the housework – but not the underlying cause of the problem.

You see, if your partner feels valued, they won't care who does the most ironing. They'll know you appreciate what they do, and that you're contributing in other ways. The housework thing really isn't the point. You need to consider the whole question of how to help your partner feel valued. That's the biggie. The housework might be one small part of that – but actually, if you can resolve the underlying cause, you may well find it stops mattering who does which bits of cleaning and cooking and shopping.

> **BELOW THE WATERLINE THERE'S A MUCH BIGGER PROBLEM LURKING**

People who can't find an answer may not want one

A colleague of mine was always saying he wanted a change of career. He started saying it when we worked together and he was still saying it when I moved on two years later. And five years after that. To begin with I tried to be supportive. I made suggestions – he was asking for them – about things he'd be qualified at, good at, enjoy and so on. But whatever I suggested, he came up with a reason why it wouldn't be possible. The money wouldn't be enough, his qualifications wouldn't count for anything, there were no suitable employers in the area. And so on.

After a while I realised that he didn't really want to move at all. So I gave up making suggestions. He kept talking about it and asking for my ideas, but I delicately avoided putting any forward.

This is a pattern commonly known as 'Yes, but...'.[11] Whatever you suggest, the other person knocks it back with some reason why it won't work. One of the problems with this is that it can leave you feeling frustrated because you want to be helpful but you seem unable to. This is demoralising with a colleague, but that's nothing to how you can feel if you routinely play this game with a close member of your family.

In fact, in one way you are being more helpful than you realise. The object of the exercise in the other person's mind (not necessarily consciously) is actually to be able to rebut all your suggestions. So by feeding them a steady stream of ideas they can reject, you're giving them just what they want. Whether it's good for their psyche in the long term is another matter.

---

[11] I must give credit here to Eric Berne MD who first identified this 'game'.

So, you want me to tell you why anyone would ask for suggestions just so they can reject them. Well, people are complicated, and 'Yes, but...' can fulfil any one (or more) of several needs. I have known people who play this game frequently in order to gain sympathy for their impossible predicament. One thing you'll notice when you get dragged into a 'Yes, but...' session is that it can go on for a while, and all that time the attention is firmly on the person who initiated it. Yep, it can be an effective attention-seeking ploy. Although I should emphasise that the perpetrator is very rarely, in my experience, conscious of what they're doing – at least not fully.

Another reason for 'Yes, butting' is because it removes responsibility for the decision from the person making it and puts it on to you. When you fail to come up with a viable suggestion (which is your job), then it's you that has failed and not them. Besides, it's not their fault if they can't reach a satisfactory resolution when you have clearly shown that there isn't one.

Once you realise someone is playing 'Yes, but...', your best bet is to stop making suggestions. Turn it around and ask them what they think they should do. Unless it's you, of course, in which case you need to ask yourself why you're doing it.

> # IT CAN LEAVE YOU FEELING FRUSTRATED BECAUSE YOU WANT TO BE HELPFUL BUT YOU SEEM UNABLE TO

Don't tell people to move on

No one wants to be unhappy, not really. I agree some people appear to wallow in it, but only because it feels safer for them. 'He that is down need fear no fall',[12] and all that. If unhappy people struggle to climb out of their swamp, there's a reason why. Either they don't know how to, or they fear it will lead to another swamp – for example, you could feel miserable when someone close to you dies, but also think that you'd feel guilty if you weren't miserable. So all you can do is choose your swamp.

On top of this, you may have noticed that there are some emotions that people find harder to admit to than others. A lot of people will more readily tell you they feel angry than, say, depressed. They'd rather admit to a specific worry than to general anxiety. There are lots of reasons for this, some of them down to upbringing, but generally speaking people find it harder to admit to general long-term emotional struggles than to specific one-off problems, partly because they're harder to rationalise. Which obviously shouldn't be relevant, but it is.

So it's much easier to say that you are worrying about whether you can sell your house, than admit to chronic general anxiety. Easier to say you're furious with a colleague over a recent incident than to own up to long-term anger issues. Easier to admit to feeling down about the recent death of your father than to admit to being seriously depressed.

On top of this, many people have been brought up with a sense that these long-term, non-specific, apparently non-rational negative feelings are somehow a sign of weakness. So they don't want to admit to grief (except when it's very recent), loneliness, anxiety,

---

[12] Seventeenth-century poet, John Bunyan, in case you don't know the line.

depression – they feel they ought to just pull themselves out of their own swamp. But of course, they can't.

And one reason people don't talk about these feelings is because they worry that you'll tell them to buck up, move on, pull their socks up, get out and do things. Listen, if it was that simple, don't you think they'd already have done it? Those emotions don't work like that. And you telling them they have to be more positive will just exacerbate their feelings of being hopeless and pathetic when they can't do it. How's that going to help?

Even professional psychologists can find it a challenge to help people with these kind of feelings. If it was as simple as telling them to pull themselves together, the shrinks wouldn't need years of training, would they? In fact they'd be out of a job – their profession wouldn't exist. These are complex emotions we're talking about, and every case is different, so it's essential that you don't make matters worse by crassly telling people to move on after a break-up or a bereavement, or to pull themselves together when they're anxious or depressed. It might work for you, but if it worked for them they'd have done it long before they opened up to you about their deepest feelings.

> # THERE ARE SOME EMOTIONS THAT PEOPLE FIND HARDER TO ADMIT TO THAN OTHERS

Loneliness is a state of mind

I suspect that, like me, if you think about lonely people you imagine old men and women living on their own. And indeed many old people living alone do feel lonely. However, loneliness in itself isn't about your physical circumstances. It's an emotion, and it has more to do with lacking emotional closeness to other people than lacking physical proximity.

This means that some people can feel happy, fulfilled, satisfied despite very little contact with other people. Maybe because of it. Think of hermits, to take this to its logical conclusion, who are not generally perceived as miserable and lonely, because they have chosen their lifestyle themselves.

On the other hand, it also means that there are people who spend lots of their time in company but who still feel lonely regardless. They might be teenagers or pensioners, shy or gregarious, single or married – it's surprising how many people feel lonely in a marriage that lacks emotional intimacy.

I have one friend who lived on his own for years very happily. Then he met a woman, fell in love and got married. Many years later she died, and he was left alone. He told me that he felt incredibly lonely, despite being in the selfsame situation he had enjoyed living in before he met her. I asked him what exactly had changed and he told me, 'I know what I'm missing now'. He had found a closeness with his wife he'd never previously had, and he couldn't stop missing it when she was no longer there.

For a start, this should make it obvious that if someone tells you they're lonely, you won't solve their problem for them by telling them to go and join a club (although I hope by now you won't be telling anyone else what's best for them). There are some people for whom this does the trick, especially if they make close friends over time, but many for whom it doesn't make any sense at all.

Many people find it hard to admit they're lonely. If they manage to admit it, don't be surprised or disbelieving just because they've got a big family, or a busy social life, or a job dealing with people constantly. Anyone might feel lonely, regardless of their circumstances.

Equally, given this section is all about helping people, if you have a friend who seems unhappy and you don't know why, consider whether they might be lonely, regardless of their circumstances. Especially if the kids have just left home, or their marriage isn't very happy, or one of their parents has just died.

More people out there than you or I can imagine are lonely, and if we want to help, we need to present ourselves as someone they can really communicate with, not just someone to have a laugh and a joke with – although obviously that as well. Then when they need someone to talk to, and they have the confidence to open up, they'll recognise us as proper friends who can help them feel a bit less alone.

> # IT HAS MORE TO DO WITH LACKING EMOTIONAL CLOSENESS TO OTHER PEOPLE THAN LACKING PHYSICAL PROXIMITY

Give them privacy

There's a popular feeling these days that 'it's good to talk'. That the stiff upper lip approach of the past is unhealthy, and we all need to open up about our feelings more, air them, discuss them, get them out in the open.

Well, surprise, surprise, you can go too far in that direction too. It's true that being unable to talk about things can be damaging and perpetuate unhappiness, but it doesn't automatically follow that everyone must therefore talk about their feelings all the time. In fact, that has its downside too. Life is there to be lived, not to be analysed incessantly, and the happiest people I know don't focus on their feelings except in occasional times of hardship. Mostly they focus on other people, and on getting on with their day, week, year. Too much introspection can make you needy and self-centred.

Look, as with all things, you need balance, moderation. The logical opposite of not being able to discuss your feelings isn't *having* to discuss your feelings. It is being *able* to discuss them. That's a very different thing.

It's certainly important that we feel we can talk through problems, sadness, worries, fears, unhappiness, anger, grief, depression – if we want to. But we don't have to want to. And one of the most frustrating things if you're in an emotional swamp is other people putting pressure on you to talk. So please don't do this to people. Not everyone feels better for talking about everything to everyone all the time. They might feel better for talking to someone at some point, but it might not be you and it might not be now.

Some people know that talking isn't going to help right now – and maybe not at any point. Maybe they have to work through something. Maybe they have an answer and just need to steel themselves to do it – talking won't achieve anything. Maybe they don't want to think about it, and talking will focus them more, not less.

Denial is hugely underrated as an emotional state. I've heard people say, 'You've got to face up to it', but actually if someone doesn't want to face up to something, why should they? The unconscious mind usually goes into denial for a very good reason – because facing up to the reality is too hard to bear. Their denial is a safety net and if you take it away – or try to force them to remove it – you leave them more vulnerable than before. The opposite of what you were trying to achieve. Of course, there are a few people who stay in this state beyond the point where it's helping them, but if they do need help it will be professional help, not yours or mine. Usually denial is a valuable and important emotional buffer, and one it's very unwise to try to dismantle in someone else.

Think back to the bad times you've gone through. I'll bet there were times you wanted to talk and times you didn't. Friends you felt like opening up to and friends you didn't. I've had people say to me, 'You'll feel better if you talk' when I know I won't. It makes me think, 'I'll feel better if I thump you but maybe let's not do either'.

The thing that can be the most help of all, in fact, is to let someone who doesn't want to talk know that you won't encourage them to. Sometimes, if someone is going through a crisis, the most helpful thing you can say is, 'I'm happy to talk if you want to, but I won't mention the subject unless you bring it up first'. That way they can relax around you, knowing they won't be under any pressure.

TOO MUCH INTROSPECTION CAN MAKE YOU NEEDY AND SELF-CENTRED

All interactions are positive or negative

I'm often struck by the fact that, if I'm having a bit of a bad day, I can be hugely lifted by a warm smile from a stranger, or a helpful shop assistant, or a friendly word from someone I barely know. They have no idea my day's going badly, but they still help.

Occasionally in my life, like everyone, I've been through a really tough patch, and the kindness of people I barely know has been doubly appreciated because they had no need to go out of their way for me. Meanwhile, those tiny gestures from people I don't know all added up to making my day just that little bit better. Of course, that's only on the days when the people around me were being positive.

I imagine you've noticed this yourself. You may also have realised that it has an even stronger effect when you're consciously aware of it. If you register and appreciate those little acts of kindness towards you, their impact is magnified.

So have you ever thought about the effect you're having on other people? Every time you smile at a stranger, or help someone who's struggling to open a door, or say a friendly hello to someone you barely know, you're making their day better. Maybe only a tiny bit better, but it all goes in the pot with the other people who are lifting their day too. Or helps in some small way to counteract that belligerent driver or grumpy neighbour they encountered earlier. This in itself should make you feel good about yourself every time you raise someone else's day, so you both gain.

I have a friend whose philosophy is that every single interaction you have with someone leaves them feeling at least a little bit better, or a little bit worse. It's never neutral. When you start monitoring how you feel when you meet other people, you find he's absolutely right. It's almost impossible to come away from even the smallest encounter without feeling invigorated or frustrated or embarrassed or cheered or worried or guilty or positive or inadequate or reassured or ignored or amused.

And you're doing this to other people, as much as they're doing it to you. What's more, if you smile at someone, almost invariably they'll smile back, which gives you that little lift that smoothes your path through the day. In fact, once in a blue moon I smile at someone who just glares back at me. And you know what? I still feel better than I would have done if I'd glared too. I know I've done my bit, offered them a soupçon of warmth, and if they choose not to take it, it's nothing to do with me. Maybe they don't know how to receive a friendly gesture, and perhaps the hundreds of people who nonetheless offer it might slowly help them to learn.

> ## YOU'RE DOING THIS TO OTHER PEOPLE, AS MUCH AS THEY'RE DOING IT TO YOU

Not everyone wants help

This group of Rules has been about how to help other people. But it doesn't hurt to point out that just because you can help someone, that doesn't automatically mean you should. This isn't always easy, because often you know that you can make a real difference in some way.

Look, it's not just about the difference your actions make. It's also about the way it makes the other person feel. Very often your help can be the thing that makes someone feel cared about, loved, worthwhile, grateful, wanted, that they can cope. And sometimes not.

There are other things they might feel instead of – or as well as – those things. They might feel patronised, belittled, helpless, child-like, beholden. They don't want those feelings. Then again, neither do they feel comfortable rejecting you when you're trying to be kind. (Unless they're your teenage child, in which case they'll be quite at ease with it.)

Whenever you offer help, you effectively invite the other person to take out a karmic loan with you. You are offering to become their karmic creditor, which means you are in a position of power over them. Yes, I know that wasn't your intention. You just wanted to be helpful. I get that. But it makes no difference – that is simply the nature of the transaction.

That's why some people don't want you to do something that appears to make their life easier. If you look at it in that way, you should be able to understand the 'I don't want your help' mentality. For a start, it should explain why your teenager doesn't want your help, and indeed is happier than most to spell it out clearly (although we both know that tomorrow they'll come asking you for money, a lift, an off-games note, more money...).

Most people will be grateful for a one-off offer of help from a stranger when they're lost or fall over. Although if you offer to help an old lady across the road and she doesn't consider herself an old lady who needs help, she may not appreciate it. Most old ladies are polite enough to decline civilly, but you need to hear what they're saying.

We also have lots of relationships where the karmic balance tips back and forth so often that no one is counting. So long as the help goes both ways, that's just what love and friendship are about really.

You might encounter more resistance – however politely expressed – from people who can never get back into credit with you: you often help them and there's nothing you need that they can help with. This will be especially true if you already hold some kind of position of superiority over them. So don't stop helping people, but do be conscious of how they respond, and understand why a few of them reject your offers. It's not about you. It's about how it makes them feel.

> IT'S NOT ABOUT YOU.
> IT'S ABOUT HOW IT MAKES
> THEM FEEL

GETTING THEM ON YOUR SIDE

Not everyone sees things the same way you do. Your mum can't necessarily see that she needs help round the house as she gets older, your boss might not see that the budget for your project isn't big enough to do it justice, your neighbour can't see why their hedge is too high, your friend doesn't see how impractical it is for you to stay out late midweek, your colleagues don't see why a particular client needs special treatment.

Half the point of understanding how people think is so that you can persuade them to think the way you do. This section is all about how to align yourself and other people so you're both looking at things the same way, and can negotiate an agreement. It's very much *not* about how to manipulate or coerce people, however. The aim is not to get what you want at all costs, but to use your people skills to get everyone wanting the same thing.

If the other person is left feeling frustrated, cheated, emotionally bludgeoned, harrassed, pressured, manipulated or beaten, you're not doing it right. The aim is for both of you to feel happy with any decisions, and to feel that you're in it together, both in agreement.

Loyalty runs both ways

It should be a given that if you have someone's loyalty, you have them on your side. So the question is: what makes your partner, your colleague, your friend, your boss, loyal to you? Some people are by nature more instinctively loyal than others, but you can get almost anyone to show you great loyalty if you know how.

The key thing to understand is that people don't *choose* to be loyal to you. Either they feel it or they don't. I used to have a boss who insisted that his team owed him loyalty – it was part of their job. However, this simply doesn't work. It might have been their job to appear loyal, to act as a loyal person would have acted, but it simply wasn't in their power to feel loyal or disloyal. Only he could control that. What's more, if you tell someone to feel loyal when they don't, you're making an unreasonable demand of them. Which, of course, is going to push them into feeling less loyal.

Yes – less loyal. Because loyalty isn't an on/off switch. Some of your friends might have some loyalty to you, but only so far. Your partner might be utterly loyal. Your boss might be loyal up to a point, but leave you on your own if you overstep a certain line.

So, if you want loyal people around you, you have to earn that loyalty. Like it or not, it's the only thing that works. The good news is that the way you earn loyalty from other people is blindingly simple. You just have to be loyal to them. Nice and easy, eh? Accept that some people will always be easier to win over than others, and that's not right or wrong, it's just how they're made. Then take every opportunity to show your commitment to them:

- Don't gossip behind their back or pass on rumours about them.

- Stand up for them in front of 'outsiders' – people outside the family, friendship group, company, department, etc.

- Show support and sympathy where they need it.

- Don't betray confidences but, beyond that, be as open as you can and co-operate with them.

- Always treat their opinions with respect, even if you disagree with them. You can voice your view without disparaging theirs.

- Listen to them when they are passionate about a view, a complaint, an idea, a project, whatever your own thoughts on the matter.

- Show you care about them individually – remember their kids' names, or the fact they had a job interview last week.

- Be appreciative when they do something for you, whether a friend remembers your favourite meal when they cook for you, or a team member wins a contract. Don't just say 'Thanks'. Tell them why you appreciate it.

If you can do all that for the people you live with and work with, you'll find yourself surrounded by loyal people.

PEOPLE DON'T *CHOOSE* TO BE LOYAL TO YOU. EITHER THEY FEEL IT OR THEY DON'T

RULE 51

Remember the details

People want to feel that they matter, that they're important to you. If you've ever had someone forget your name who really should know it, you'll know how it makes you feel: unimportant, inconsequential, uncared about, not interesting or worthwhile enough to remember. It's a horrible feeling. When someone does remember you, you get the opposite feeling.

Of course, if all they do is remember your name, it doesn't usually count for much (apart from avoiding all those negative feelings you'd have had if they hadn't recalled it). It depends how well they know you, when you last met, and how you know each other – the CEO remembering even just your name after meeting you once two years ago would feel pretty good.

I once worked with a very well-known actor when I was young – actors meet people all the time, cast, crew, directors, and can do several jobs a year with all those new faces. I didn't expect to meet this guy again because I was doing a fill-in job on a small corporate production that only lasted a few days. As I told him (he was very chatty with everyone), I had other career plans lined up. By chance, I had a couple of weeks spare about two years later and worked for the same film company again. And it so happened this actor was back for this film too. I assumed he wouldn't remember me – how could he? – but as soon as he saw me he gave me a really warm greeting and asked why I was there and how the career plans were going. He remembered exactly what I'd been up to. I can't tell you how chuffed I was and how good it made me feel that I'd been worth remembering.

So never underestimate the value of remembering people, and the details of what they're up to, especially if they might perceive you as being senior to them in some way, or 'above' them, as I viewed my actor friend. Remember the names of the receptionist's kids, or the fact that a colleague has a big family celebration coming up, or where your neighbour is off to on holiday, or that your cousin's wife likes peppermint tea with a bit of honey in it.

Are you thinking, how the hell am I supposed to remember all that? I suspect you may be. And I'll give you two answers. Firstly, the more you are genuinely interested and engaged in the conversation, the more likely you are to remember it (that's how the actor did it – he listened to people properly). And secondly, you can write it down. Because obviously you can't be expected to remember it all in your head. I've kept countless notes on customers' files to remind me when their daughter's driving test is, or what kind of wine they like. If you know your cousin and his wife will be over again in November, set an electronic reminder of some kind for yourself.

My dentist always knows what I've been up to – holidays or trips I said I was going on when I last saw him, for example. I'm quite sure he keeps notes. Am I offended that he's 'faking' interest in me when really he has it all written down? Of course not. I'm pleased he considers me worth making notes about, and appreciate him taking the trouble. I don't care whether he remembers it in his head or on paper.

THE MORE YOU ARE
GENUINELY INTERESTED
AND ENGAGED IN
THE CONVERSATION, THE
MORE LIKELY YOU ARE TO
REMEMBER IT

RULE 52

Flattery should never be empty

I know someone who used to do a bit of fortune telling, tarot card reading, astrology – you know the sort of thing – to earn some money on the side. He had a list of things he could say to people which made them feel he'd really got the measure of them, but in fact you could say them to absolutely anyone. One of these was, 'Ah! I see you're not easily won over by flattery...'. I particularly loved the irony of this one, which apparently used to go unnoticed by everyone on the receiving end of it.

If you look up flattery in a dictionary, you'll see that it means excessive or insincere praise. Which makes the phrase 'empty flattery' almost meaningless, since the whole point is that flattery is empty praise.[13] Some people will lap up any kind of flattery, while others recognise it for what it is and resent the insincerity. Even if you know you're dealing with the first type, you're still in effect lying to them if you give them praise you don't really mean.

You don't want to get caught out bestowing shallow and false praise on anyone, by them or by the people listening. You will come across as lacking integrity at best, and at worst you could get hoist with your own petard later ('I wanted to give you my latest painting because you loved it so much. You can hang it on your living room wall.')

Of course, praising people is a valuable way of building loyalty and helping you both to feel you're on the same side. It shows consideration and care for the other person and it can encourage them to keep doing the stuff they're doing well. And it can just

---

[13] So I suppose 'empty flattery' would logically be insincere insincerity. Is that like a double negative – in which case empty flattery means genuine praise? Or is it just tautologous? (Don't write in.)

make them feel good about themselves, regardless of any benefit to you. Just because this group of Rules is about getting people on your side, it doesn't mean you can't also act altruistically.

So don't stop giving praise. But do make sure that you really mean what you say. Never allow genuine praise to turn into empty flattery or everyone loses out. My family has quite a few actors in it, and it's a persistent actor worry what to say to a friend when you've been to see them in a show that you didn't like. You go round backstage afterwards and you have to say something. In all the after-show buzz it's really not a good time to give them notes on how to improve. The answer to this quandary – and any similar situation you may face – is to find something you enjoyed and just focus on that: 'Darling, you spoke your lines wonderfully!' (which could mean a lot of things, frankly) or 'What a beautiful looking production!' or even 'I can't believe you managed to learn all those lines – what a huge part. However did you do it?' In other words sound positive, but without saying anything you don't actually mean.

> # PRAISING PEOPLE IS A VALUABLE WAY OF BUILDING LOYALTY

Praise effectively

While we're on the subject of praise (if you're reading this in order[14]), not all praise is the same. Not even all genuine praise. It's probably fair to say that genuine praise isn't ever a bad thing, but there's OK praise and then there's really great praise. People who understand how to give really great praise are relatively rare, and they're wonderful. And you can be one of them once you know how.

So here's a quick lesson for you in how to give people the best possible praise. Ten out of ten praise (that's your score, not theirs).

The first, and perhaps most important thing, is to make the praise specific. Don't just say, 'Well done' or 'That was brilliantly organised'. You can start there, but then tell them exactly why: 'Not only did it all go smoothly, but you stayed cheerful and unruffled throughout, and you thought of everything, right down to the well-chosen flowers and the personal taxis waiting for people at the end.' Now isn't that better to hear than a simple 'well done'? There's nothing pat or dismissive about it. You've obviously really noticed and appreciated how hard they worked and what their personal contribution was.

Now discuss it with them. Ask them questions. People love talking about themselves, and it shows you're really interested. 'Where did you find that great slide to illustrate your volcano analogy? Did you put it together yourself?'

And here's another point you'll recognise if you've ever been on the receiving end: don't add a 'but': 'Next time let's try to keep it down to fifteen minutes.' Any kind of sting in the tail devalues the praise that went before it. You can't score ten out of ten that way.

---

[14] Not everyone does, you know. It's good to break out of your comfort zone – why don't you try hopping around the book for a change? Just to see how you cope!

You're up to about six out of ten already. In fact, you may already have scored full marks for minor items of praise – your young child's picture they've brought home from school, or a minor success at work (it can start sounding insincere and patronising if you make a huge deal out of a small thing). But when someone has scored a particular triumph, there's still more you can do.

People like recognition. There are lots of different reasons for wanting it, but everyone does. So when someone does really well, make your praise more formal or more public – and let them know. Put it on their personnel record, send them an email of thanks and copy other people in the family or company in on it. Thank them in front of people whose good opinion they value. Tell them when other people praise them: 'Meg was telling me she couldn't have got through her wedding without your calming influence, and your ability to know exactly what was supposed to be happening everywhere at any time.'

So there you are. You now have the wherewithal to be a ten out of ten praiser. And the delightful privilege alongside it of being able to give other people a palpable sense of being valued and appreciated.

> PEOPLE WHO UNDERSTAND
> HOW TO GIVE REALLY GREAT
> PRAISE ARE RELATIVELY RARE,
> AND THEY'RE WONDERFUL

Keep your praise in proportion

You'd think, wouldn't you, that if praise is a good thing, lots of praise must be an even better thing. Strangely, though, that really isn't the case. It's unexpectedly damaging to give people disproportionate praise. This is at its worst with children whose parents are always telling them how clever they are and how fantastic everything they do is. That's because parents are a huge influence and the child is still developing. But it's still true when it comes to praising your friends or your team or your family.

I'm not saying you shouldn't give praise often. Give it as often as it's due. Just don't give too much of it. For a start, praising someone beyond what's due can be patronising, and can also make it sound insincere. Saying 'That's brilliant, well done! You're amazing!' to someone just because they picked up some milk on the way home simply isn't convincing. I know that some of us are more given to this kind of language than others, and it might be that your friends and colleagues all know that a 'Thank you *so much*! You're fabulous!' from you is the equivalent of a 'Cool, cheers' from someone else. Up to a point this is fine, we're all different. Although it does make me think of one person I know whose effusiveness dial is permanently set to full, and other people do find him extremely patronising.

The bigger problem with over-praising (and this is where parents can unwittingly create huge problems) is that it sets people up to fail, and that makes them anxious. Deep down, they know perfectly well that they're not that good or special, so they have to put themselves under increasing pressure to live up to your praise. Besides, if you give someone glowing praise for every little achievement, you've devalued the currency. You've left yourself nowhere to go when they do something that really is exceptional.

My wife once organised a big family event. She's good at that sort of thing. Very good. Lots of people told her afterwards how amazingly she'd done and how fantastically smoothly everything went and well done for pulling it all together. She felt slightly frustrated by this, although everyone's intention was to make her feel good about herself. We talked about it and she told me, 'It's as though they thought it was a real achievement, but I thought it was easy. If they think that's a stretch for me, I'm disappointed by their low opinion of me.' What she wanted to hear was: 'That was superbly organised, which is no more than I'd expect from you.' Now that would have felt like real praise.

Another option is to thank people instead of praising them. My wife was completely happy with the people who thanked her for doing such a good job. After all, she wanted recognition, and this gave it to her without being patronising.

Once you think all this through, you should be able to keep your praise in proportion. If in doubt, however – or even if not in doubt – the trick is to spend less time making general statements such as 'Well done!' and more time picking out specific details and discussing them, as per the last Rule. That will be really rewarding for them without you having to make a decision about how high to set the praise-o-meter.

> # IF YOU GIVE SOMEONE GLOWING PRAISE FOR EVERY LITTLE ACHIEVEMENT, YOU'VE DEVALUED THE CURRENCY

RULE 55

People want to be liked

This sounds like a truism, which of course it is. With very rare exceptions such as clinically diagnosable sociopaths – who I'm not going to advise on without professional qualifications – people would rather be liked than not liked. Some people are desperate to be liked at all costs, and some prefer to be liked but don't let it get in the way. No, actually, even these people care quite a lot about being liked by the people they themselves like and respect – they're just more discriminating than the former category. Obviously it's a spectrum and not just two groups, and it's useful to be aware of where on the spectrum the people you deal with are placed.

Everyone recognises, consciously or otherwise, that liking is generally reciprocal. You don't often like someone who really dislikes you. So people are more likely to co-operate with you if they think you like them than if they think you don't. After all, what have they got to lose by being obstructive if you don't like them anyway? Whereas if you like each other, it will take more for them to get in the way of that.

So the Rule here is that if you like someone you're more likely to get the best from them than if you don't. They'll sense that you like them – come on, you can pretty much tell who likes you and who doesn't – and that will encourage them to retain your good opinion.

If this sounds like it's too simple, think about the cantankerous people you know, the ones who don't seem to like people much. They clearly haven't worked it out. If they liked you a bit more, wouldn't you be more inclined to be supportive when they asked for it? More likely to agree with them? More likely to listen to them when they wanted to be heard?

Of course, the other person has to be aware that you like them. Which probably happens naturally if you do – all of this runs smoothly most of the time and neither of you needs to give it any conscious thought. But what about the people you actually don't like? They're the pesky blighters to deal with, aren't they? And the fact you don't like them, and they sense it, means they probably don't give you any more help than they need to. So you don't like them even more, and look – here's a vicious circle.

Now, you don't have to break this circle if you don't want to, but surely you do want to? You need to start liking this irritating, difficult, obstructive person if you want to get the best out of them. Tricky, eh? Yes, it is tricky, but it isn't impossible.

I find the best approach is not to try to like the whole of them all at once – it's just too difficult. But there's almost always something to like. You just have to look for it. Think about what their partner or kids must see in them, consider why they are as they are. Even if you begin simply by feeling sorry for them which, as Shakespeare said, is 'a degree to love'. Perhaps they're good at their job which makes your life easier, or they can be very funny, or they're kind to animals – I don't know, but if you make a start, it's often possible to reach a point where you stop disliking them and, slowly, move into liking them. And as for them being able to tell – pay them the occasional genuine compliment, give them a smile when you see them, and it will come naturally over time.

YOU DON'T OFTEN LIKE SOMEONE WHO REALLY DISLIKES YOU

Earn their respect

OK, that last Rule goes the other way too. People are more likely to help and support you if they like you. But some people don't seem to like you, so it's harder for you to get them on your side. They may not be deliberately scuppering your plans (the next bit of the book is about people who are particularly difficult), but neither are they going out of their way to help.

You're not going to get these people to like you by baking them cakes and flattering them and giving them flowers and generally trying too hard. In fact, other than treating them as your normal Rules self, there's no point trying to get them to like you at all. That's because what you really need from these people is respect (and trying too hard will cost you respect). It's very hard to dislike someone you respect – unless they're actually unpleasant. Which you're not, because you're a Rules player and always treat other people decently. Someone you respect may not be your best friend, but you'll like them well enough. That's well enough to be helpful and supportive if they ask. If someone respects you they'll value your approval, so they won't lightly risk it by being unco-operative or difficult with you.

If you ask, you'll get lots of advice on how to earn respect, but it all boils to this:

- Be good at what you do.

- Know you are good at it.

- Do it with integrity.

Whether it's at work or among your friends or at the local club you help run, make sure you're good at your job. That doesn't only mean meeting your deadlines or hitting your targets, because to do your job really well you must also achieve your aims with calmness and grace and without fuss or making unreasonable demands of other people. Got it? You don't just do the job well on paper – you do it well in terms of your interactions with other people too.

The reason you have to know you're good at what you do is because you won't earn respect if you keep asking for approval and recognition and confirmation – either verbally or in unspoken ways. You'll just look needy.

And as for integrity – always adhere to your values, even when it might be easier not to. Uphold what you believe in in little ways and – if necessary – in bigger ways. Always treat other people with respect and decency, and stand up for them if they need your backup.

Do all of that – which shouldn't be so hard – and it will be well-nigh impossible for people not to respect you. And once they respect you, it's easier for them to like you than not.

> # TO DO YOUR JOB REALLY WELL, YOU MUST ALSO ACHIEVE YOUR AIMS WITH CALMNESS AND GRACE

RULE 57

Have a sense of humour

This is a big part of being liked and respected. It's easy to like someone with a sense of humour, so getting people to support you is bound to be easier. If you can make someone laugh, you've pretty much hooked them.

This doesn't mean, however, that you should go around the office or wherever asking, 'Have you heard the one about...?' You don't need to be a joker, or count how many belly laughs you manage to get out of other people each day. I'm not talking about that kind of humour.

And let's get the other things I'm not talking about out of the way while we're here. Certain types of humour are off limits to Rules players:

- anything that makes someone else in the group/family/ organisation the butt of the joke...

- ...which includes any kind of practical jokes that make someone else the butt (which is basically all practical jokes to be honest)

- anything that is offensive to minority social groups – sexism, racism, jokes against disabled people and so on.

Making fun of people who aren't part of the group is still ultimately not a very kind thing to do, and won't make you a likeable joker. They'll make you an unlikeable one. The only exception I can think of to this is satire, which pokes fun at people who have chosen to put themselves in the public eye. So you're allowed to make (acceptable) jokes about the incumbent Prime Minister or President if you like.

So what does that leave you with? Well, there's a whole raft of humour along the lines of witticisms, surreal connections, clever puns, irony...This is either your natural style or it isn't. If it is, that's great. Go for it. However, if it isn't, it's not really a thing you can learn. Humour is extremely personal.

Fortunately, however, there is one branch of humour that we can all master, and it's the one that will make you more likeable than any other: self-deprecation. We can all make ourselves the butt of the joke, and tell stories that make us look a bit daft, or where we poke fun at ourselves. You don't have to plan a set number of self-deprecating remarks a day – just do your best to grab the opportunities when they come along. Even if it doesn't arise that often, people will appreciate your ability to laugh at yourself, and to allow them to laugh along with you.

There's only one small proviso to this, and that is that you don't want to undermine your own credibility in the group. In the main this won't arise, but if you were persistently to come into work and relate how your total lack of forward planning had caused this or that humorous situation at home, eventually people might start to wonder why you're being employed as project manager.

> # HUMOUR IS EXTREMELY
> # PERSONAL

Don't be scared to admit your mistakes

I used to work for a boss who would occasionally tell a story about his early days in the business. This was a guy I respected enormously, who was very talented, and good at listening to everyone else too. He never issued edicts from on high – his was always a collaborative approach. In one of these stories, he would talk about how he'd absolutely insisted that a particular product line was a hopeless idea, and recommended it be dropped. However, his colleagues overruled him, and the product turned out to be the most successful line they'd ever had at that time. He finished by saying how lucky it was they didn't listen to him.

What is interesting about this is my reaction to the story. Here's what I *didn't* think: 'What a loser, that's a stupid mistake to make. How did he get to where he is today?' Yet, that's the reaction many people fear if they own up to mistakes, past or recent. However, it's not how your listeners really react at all. What did I actually think when I heard this story? I thought: 'What a nice guy. I know his judgement is sound, so it's unusual for him to make such a mistake. But how humble to admit it when he does. It makes him seem very human and, after all, I know myself that no one is infallible.'

And the very fact the man himself was comfortable with talking about his mistake made me feel he'd understand if I made mistakes when I was working for him. It was reassuring to know we're all capable of the odd misjudgement.

Another place I've encountered this is among parents, where it's so refreshing to hear someone admit to some ludicrously bad parenting decision. Not just the disingenuous minor and irrelevant moments, but the more significant mistakes. I once asked a parent what I should feed her child on a playdate. She replied,

'God knows. He's a ridiculously picky eater. It's all my own fault – I pandered to him far too much when he was younger.' I liked her hugely for it.

So why do some of us resist admitting to our mistakes? Lots of us in fact. Well, the thing that set this guy apart was his confidence. He knew he'd learned from his mistake, and he knew his judgement was good, so he could afford a chink in his armour, knowing the rest of it was intact. Those of us who hate admitting to mistakes are generally less confident. We fear people will think we really are that stupid, or inexperienced, or blind, or generally fallible the rest of the time.

The trouble is that if we can't admit to a mistake, we come across as defensive. If we never admit to them, we're depriving ourselves of the chance to look human and generous and humble. Isn't that a mistake in itself?

I don't advocate broadcasting every tiny error or slip-up to the family or the office or the world at large. But once in a while – especially when you catch yourself about to tie yourself in knots to avoid confessing – just reflect on all the positives of just holding up your hands and saying, 'I've no idea what I was thinking. Just look what I've done. Duh!'

> # IF WE CAN'T ADMIT TO
> # A MISTAKE, WE COME ACROSS
> # AS DEFENSIVE

RULE 59

Be tolerant

I used to work with a guy who sang loudly to himself at his desk, which was in the same office as mine. Friendly guy, always cheerful (hence the singing), but he drove me mad with frustration. I found it really hard to concentrate on my work. When I tried to discuss it, he couldn't see it from my perspective, and thought I should just cheer up and enjoy it.

Now, this wasn't the most empathetic response he could have made, but he did sort of have a point. Because I've found over the years that the biggest problem with irritating people is me. It's my response. When someone sings at their desk, or is always bragging, or makes snide comments, or talks endlessly, or never says no to their kids, I feel irritated and frustrated. At this point I have two options, and I always used to pick the wrong one (I'm getting better these days).

The first – and wrong – option is to fight it. To keep wishing they'd stop, to get wound up, to moan about them. When you do that, you're always on edge, waiting for them to do the annoying thing again. You're forever on the look-out so you can say 'See? I told you it was infuriating . . .' to yourself, inside your head. Which is pointless. The effect is to damage relations between the two of you, because you can't help but show your dislike of their behaviour on some level, whether overtly or not.

So what's the alternative? Quite simply, you have to accept that this person has an irritating habit, and you can't change it. The only thing you can change is yourself. So stop fighting it. Now you can actually start to deal with your reaction to it. For one thing, you can think about why they do it, and try to empathise. Or just see the positives. My singing colleague was ever cheerful – in a maddening way, but actually it probably beats sharing an office with a misery guts.

Now you've stopped fighting, you can think about whether some of this is actually your stuff. Does everyone else find them as irritating as you? If not, perhaps they push your buttons for a particular reason. I struggle, for example, with people who do things slowly, because I'm very impatient. That's my stuff more than theirs, really.

Here's another thing you can do once you accept the irritation: minimise the frustration. I should have worn earplugs, or listened to music, or planned my most focused work for when my colleague was out of the office.

My wife and I have a couple of friends who we compare notes about after we see them, to see who has spotted the best example of their irritating habit (appeasing their kids, or putting their partner down in public, for example). Not only do we find it makes their frustrating habit entertaining rather than irritating, but also we are almost willing them to do it (I don't recommend doing this bitchily with a wide group of people – keep it private with just your partner or a very close friend).

All these methods of ameliorating the problem won't exist until you accept it and move on. Along with the best option of all – hard to master but well worth a try: just ignore it. (I mean really ignore it, not just self-righteously try to catch yourself ignoring it. We've all done that.)

> # THE ONLY THING YOU CAN CHANGE IS YOURSELF

RULE 60

Make individual relationships

We all tend to like and trust people we see as 'our own kind'. That's because we know where we are with them. In the case of family and close friends, we can generally take it as read, but it can take some work on your part when it comes to people you don't choose[15] – colleagues, other parents at the school gate, passing acquaintances, clients, neighbours, your sister-in-law's aunt.

It's worth having a good relationship with these people, though. Quite apart from wanting to spread a little happiness generally, there are times when you want these people on your side. So it can only help if you can show them that you're one of them. That you share their likes or dislikes, or have the same worries as them, or come from the same part of the world, or enjoy the same movies.

I'm not suggesting you fake any of this. Regardless of any ethical considerations, it just doesn't work. People can tell and it will make them more mistrustful. But listen, we all have something in common with just about everyone. You just have to look for it. Sometimes you don't even have to look very hard – they might be wearing clothing that proclaims their favourite football team or hobby. Or they might have a poster pinned up on their wall. All you have to do is comment: 'You're a Man U supporter? I'm a Chelsea man myself. Did you see the match last Saturday?' . . . and you're off. Don't bore them with it every time you meet, but refer to it occasionally to remind you both that you have a connection.

It's not always that obvious, of course. Sometimes you have to work for it. But if you ask people questions about themselves, and

---

[15] OK, sometimes family might fall into this bracket too.

listen to the answers, you'll almost always find something, in my experience. For me it can often be kids – mine are spread over a wide age range so I can empathise with a parent of young kids and with grandparents. Other people have an instinct for sniffing out fellow classic car enthusiasts, or gardeners, or *Lord of the Rings* fans.

Keep looking until you find something. If they're off to pick up their child from swimming, mention you have a child that loves swimming too. If they mention they won't be around next week because they're on holiday, ask where they're going. It might be somewhere you love too.

It's a great feeling when you find a link with someone you hadn't previously felt any sense of familiarity with. So keep it going. Let them know you appreciate it. Don't harp on it like a stuck record, but do refer to it from time to time, and build on it if you can. Have the odd private exchange – not anything that excludes others, but make them feel you don't have this same bond with everyone. Which indeed you don't.

Actually, do have this bond with everyone you can – but make it different in every case. It can turn acquaintances into friends, and isn't that even better?

> # IT'S A GREAT FEELING WHEN YOU FIND A LINK WITH SOMEONE

RULE 61

Turn the best side to the front

This Rule is about creating a sense of empathy, like the last one. Humans are social animals and we want to make that social connection with other people. The more you can help this along, the more people you will find you have on your side. Whether you want to beg a favour, close a sale, drive social change, come to an agreement, get someone to sign your petition, organise a lift share rota or politely ask a neighbour to keep their dog off your front garden, the more empathy you have with the other person, the better your chances of success.

This Rule can be slightly tricky to get your head around until you get in the swing of it. Some people – if you're lucky you'll be one of them – do it intuitively without even realising it. Most of us have to make a conscious effort. At least until we get used to it.

I had a colleague who was just brilliant at it. We had a wide range of clients, from all classes and backgrounds. And this colleague of mine would subtly change the way she spoke to each of them. It wasn't a huge change – most people would never have noticed it – but she would be a little bit more formal with this client, or more matey with that one, or more deferential, or more distant here, or less chatty there.

The crucial thing (and this is why it can take a little while to master) is that she wasn't faking any of it. She wasn't a distant person sometimes pretending to be chatty, or a matey person faking being respectful. These were all different sides of her real self, and she simply presented the most appropriate side to each person she encountered.

This is about subtle behaviours. It's about choosing a particular form of address, or choosing a suitable turn of phrase. Look, we all swear, don't we? Your worst swear word might be way less bad than someone else's, but it's still swearing to you, however mild the next person might think it. Or maybe you're big into swearing. Whatever. Now, think of the worst, sweariest thing you'd personally ever say, if you were with your best friend or your partner or whoever you are most able to be yourself round. OK, whatever that word is, think of someone you'd never say it in front of. Your grandfather? Your MD? A customer you've never met before? Your 5-year-old?

Right, that's what I'm talking about. It's the same you, but you'd say the Bad Word in front of one person and not in front of another. And this Rule is about presenting a different side of you to different people. You might call one person sir or madam, and the next by their first name, despite being in the same relation to them both. You know person A likes to be treated with deference, and person B enjoys feeling like an equal.

If you're switched on to the people you're dealing with, the way they speak and behave, the phrases they use and the attitudes they have, you can adapt your own behaviour to sit comfortably with theirs. They'll appreciate it without even realising it.

MOST OF US HAVE TO MAKE A CONSCIOUS EFFORT. AT LEAST UNTIL WE GET USED TO IT

People generally agree with themselves

People are much more likely to go along with you if you do things their way. I realise that doesn't always suit you, but it's important to recognise it. Once someone has proposed – or even overtly backed – an idea, it's much harder for them to work against it. They'll lose face if it doesn't work out, so it's in their interests to buy into it.

Sometimes you'll be pleased, impressed, convinced, taken with someone else's idea and happy to do things their way. Excellent. Other times you find yourself at loggerheads with someone, and you can see that if you push your approach through regardless, they simply won't co-operate. They might even try to undermine you, to prove their point that your way was the wrong way.

There are several options here. The one most people overlook is the possibility that the other person might be right. Or at least that they might not be any less right than you – there's more than one good way to go about most things. Why not do it their way? If you want a holiday on the beach doing very little, and your partner wants to hire a narrow boat on the canals for a week, maybe you should let them pick the holiday this time. You can agree you get to choose next time, and you never know, narrow-boating might be more fun than you ever thought.

The next option of course, where you really are sure you're right, is to use all your persuasive powers to get the other person to buy into your idea. Show them why it will be in their interests as well as yours – it will be less work, or make them look good, or be a stimulating challenge, or give them a chance to work in a particular team, or get them noticed by the high-ups. Even if you have the authority to impose your idea on others, it's always more effective to get them on board willingly.

There are two parts to every project: the destination, and the route you take to get there. If you are adamant that your idea is the only one that will work – and you have the authority to impose it on your team, your family, your fellow club members, your kids, your friends – at least give them a chance to determine how you'll collectively achieve it. If someone in your team doesn't think it's a smart move to exhibit at a particular trade show, but you're not budging because you know you're right, put them in charge of the exhibition stand display and give them free rein. I mean properly stand back and don't interfere, just be there if they ask for support. OK, maybe they're useless at that sort of thing. In that case, hand over all the logistics to them, or the advance promotion – hey, you'll think of something. The point is that you've given them something to buy into so they feel a good performance reflects well on them. Being a good Rules player, you'll be sure to give them credit when it all goes swimmingly. And when the whole exhibition is a resounding success you'll never, ever say 'I told you so'.

> **THERE ARE TWO PARTS TO EVERY PROJECT: THE DESTINATION, AND THE ROUTE YOU TAKE TO GET THERE**

RULE 63

Credit people with your own ideas

Here's another way to get people on board. I said in the last Rule that people will always buy into their own ideas, so you need to take that and run with it. If you break that down a bit further, you could say that people will always buy into ideas that they *believe* are their own. So logically you should be able to get someone on board with almost any idea, if you can get them to believe that it's theirs.

When this works, everyone wins. You're happy because your idea is the one being taken up. They're happy because as far as they're concerned their idea is the one being taken up. What's not to like?

I should point out that this strategy is a subtle one, and it works best in the early stages of planning. It's no good thinking that you can fall out big time with someone over a clash of ideas, and then suddenly convince them that your idea was really theirs. This is more about identifying people early on who could be dissenting voices, and getting them on side right from the start. Which is always the happiest way to go about things.

I know a chair of school governors who finds this approach invaluable. In a non-executive role, her job is all about trying to find consensus and agreement between a disparate group of people. It doesn't help the school's senior management if the board of governors is disunited. So she brings this strategy into play when there's a strategic decision coming up which she knows one of the governors is likely to resist.

So how's it done? It's all about credit. Once you give someone credit for an idea, preferably in front of other people, it's very hard for them to say, 'That wasn't my idea'. Especially if they're not entirely sure that it wasn't. You can't be heavy-handed about this – you need them to believe it was their idea. So listen out for anything they say that you can pick up on and turn around. Suppose the school is considering expanding, and one governor who is maybe naturally averse to change says, 'Taking on more pupils is going to make the place feel less like a school family and more like a university'. You can respond by saying, 'I quite agree, and actually as our students get older they need to expand their horizons and prepare for university. That's a really good point, thank you.'

Another way of doing this is to tell someone, 'Funnily enough, it was that point you made last week that made me realise what a good idea this was...' Or, 'That's a really good idea, and what if we also...' You can't put words in someone's mouth, but you can take something they say and develop it into what you'd like them to believe.

Be careful, be subtle, and remember that it only works if they come out of it feeling good about themselves.

> # ONCE YOU GIVE SOMEONE CREDIT FOR AN IDEA, IT'S VERY HARD FOR THEM TO SAY, 'THAT WASN'T MY IDEA.'

Don't tell them they're wrong (even if they are)

Getting people on your side should be fairly straightforward when they're sitting on the fence. So long as you're right, it shouldn't be too hard to persuade them over to you. But what happens when they're firmly on the other side of the fence? When they're holding a position that is completely incompatible with yours?

First of all, as we saw a couple of Rules back, you need to consider the possibility that they might be right. But what if they're not? What if you're absolutely certain they're wrong, and you need to talk them – along with the rest of the group – round to your way of thinking? You want everyone on side for the plan, project, scheme, idea to work. However, telling someone else they're wrong doesn't generally go down very well.

Look, we all know they're wrong,[16] but the aim is not to make them feel stupid. How will that help? The aim is to keep them on board despite expressing the opposite view from them. You can't expect that to work if you call a spade a spade. You don't have to call a spade a fork, but would it really hurt you to call it a hand-held earth-moving tool?

Think about it from their perspective. If you come at them head-on with your disagreement, they'll have two choices: to back down, or dig their heels in. If they back down, the likelihood is they'll still passively resist you, which amounts to the same thing as becoming entrenched anyway. That's not what you want, is it? So you need to offer them a wider choice. Give them another route. Sidle up to them and gently steer them in a better direction.

---

[16] I'm trusting you here. If you say they're wrong, they're wrong.

There are lots of Rules about how to be persuasive, but your immediate problem is how do you point out they're wrong without telling them, 'You're wrong'? You have to find a way of making it clear you're on the other side of the fence without putting their back up. Give them a way to concede the point without losing face. It starts with simple words. Phrasing your opposition in a way that feels co-operative and not combative. Here are a few examples of things to say which won't inflame the situation:

- 'That's not right' (simple, but so much better than 'that's wrong'). A lot of people prefer to soften it a bit: 'That can't be right, can it?', 'I don't think that's right', 'I'm not sure that's right', etc., etc.

- 'I don't agree with you' (so the emphasis is on you not agreeing, not on them being wrong).

- 'I look at it differently', or, 'I don't see it like that'.

- 'The facts suggest a different story to me'.

- 'You're right about one thing' (find some tiny point to agree on and then put your point of view).

The tone with which you say these things needs to match the words, of course. You don't want to be so hesitant or nervous you don't make your point clearly. Nor do you want to sound aggressive or patronising. Be assertive and conciliatory at the same time. Master that, and you'll go a long way to defusing arguments and creating a way for the other person to change their position.

> ## SIDLE UP TO THEM AND GENTLY STEER THEM IN A BETTER DIRECTION

Get them to collaborate

You really want a spirit of collaboration in your work team, your club or society, your family, your neighbourhood group. When everyone works positively together, the group dynamic tends to keep just about everyone on side, and by definition a collaborative group will all be working to the same shared ends. If you're at the bottom of the ladder at work, your ability to achieve this may be limited, but, as soon as you have any managerial role, you can put it into practice. Meanwhile you can aim for collaboration in your family and any non-work groups you're involved in.

There are lots of useful strategies for getting everyone to work together, but the key one is very simple: set collective goals rather than individual ones, and give collective rewards. The whole team needs to perform well, and then the whole team will be rewarded together. There's still room for individual praise and rewards too (so long as they're not competitive within the team), but the emphasis should be on the collective effort.

Once everyone has grasped this central idea, it's much easier to get them working together on a daily basis. It's a logical progression, so all you have to do is encourage it. Here are a few ways you can do that:

- Include everyone in making important decisions.

- Be flexible about roles – the important thing is to exploit everyone's strengths.

- Practise what you preach: share credit, rewards, fun tasks with the rest of the group. Don't hog the best bits.

- Encourage people to share knowledge so they understand where each other fit in to the group.

- Don't judge people for bad ideas and suggestions. Demonstrate that all ideas are welcome. (Yes, I know some of them will be daft. You don't have to use them. But that person's next idea might be genius. Only they might never suggest it if they were made to feel stupid over the last one.)

If you're in charge of a group that can subdivide, let people choose their own teams. This might be training groups within your local swimming club, or pairs of family members doing chores, or sub-groups within a big project at work. The fact is that people will be happier and more co-operative if they collaborate with the people they want to. We're all different, and some people will always rub others up the wrong way. You can't stop that happening, no matter how motivational and collaborative you are when you're running the show. You can still have a collaborative overall group. In fact, that's much easier with happy sub-teams. If everyone wants to do well, they'll opt for groupings that will work. They'll get that they need an organiser on their team, or someone who understands programming, or whatever it is. Left to their own devices, people who want to succeed don't just choose to work with their best mates. Trust them, and they'll sort themselves into productive and effective teams pretty much every time. And be happier for it.

SET COLLECTIVE GOALS RATHER THAN INDIVIDUAL ONES

Be human

When you're in a position of authority, it's tempting to come across as all-powerful. After all, you want to command respect. So you might be a very benign omnipotent being, but you still like to seem in control all the time, however nicely.

That is a bit scary though, isn't it? Being around God is quite daunting, however loving your god is. And if you're an all-knowing manager or teacher or dad or expert in your field, you're not someone other people can relax around. More to the point, you're not someone they feel needs their support. You can clearly cope regardless, so what could they possibly add?

I met someone only the other day who was like this. She knew exactly what she was doing, why she was doing it, what she needed and where she was going. She was completely in control of her programme of nurturing and listening to people. She was absolutely terrifying, and I didn't particularly warm to her. If she'd said she'd needed my help, I wouldn't have believed her. She didn't need anyone's help.

And yet you know that you *do* need people on your side. There are plenty of projects that won't succeed, arguments you can't win, jobs you can't complete, without their support. So it doesn't make sense to come across as needing no one and nothing.

Obviously you can go too far in the other direction. That's why most of us are more inclined to appear entirely self-sufficient. You'd be quite right in thinking that it's a bad idea to appear needy and unable to manage. That's not going to inspire confidence in anyone else. And if you're in any kind of position of leadership, it's important that your people know they can trust you, that you'll look after them, that you know what you're doing.

So you need to strike a balance here. Don't be all vulnerable and look as if you can't cope. But don't come across as the 'perfect' leader either – never wrong, never flawed, always in control. This applies whether you're the boss, mum or dad, the chair of a local organisation, or anything else. Look at other people around you in these kinds of positions. The very best ones do command confidence and respect, but they manage to be human as well.

So show your human side. Tell the occasional joke against yourself. If you're a manager, talk about your family once in a while, or keep a photo of the kids on your desk. Ask the occasional favour – nothing too significant or demanding. Just enough to show you aren't completely in control all the time, and you need the other person's help for everything to run smoothly. Don't try to be a benign deity. Aim to come across as a highly competent human.

> ## IT DOESN'T MAKE SENSE TO COME ACROSS AS NEEDING NO ONE AND NOTHING

Share

I grew up with a friend whose mum would never tell him what was going on until she had to. She seemed to think that parenting should operate on a need-to-know basis. In many ways she was a great mum – patient, fun, loving – but it drove my mate crazy that she would spring things on him at the last minute, or organise things behind his back. As he got older she'd ask him to do things around the house. If anything was unusual he tended to ask why he was doing it ('Why are we moving the table out of the kitchen?', 'What do you need me to buy eggs for at this time of night?', and the like), but she played her cards close to her chest. She was full of phrases like 'What you don't know won't hurt you,' or 'Curiosity killed the cat'.

The result of this, over time, was that my friend never really felt like a fully paid up member of his own family. On the one hand it kind of amused him, but on another level he felt excluded. What's more, he'd usually find out eventually what was going on, or why the kitchen table had been moved, and often he could see a much better way of doing it. But it was too late to suggest it by then.

You get the message. People want to feel involved and included. They work better when they understand what their efforts are supposed to achieve, and they can't help you improve things if they have no idea what you're trying to do. How can you get any-one on your side when they don't know what your side is?

I'm sure you're not as secretive as my friend's mother was. She was partly a product of her generation, and it's easy to exclude your kids when they're small, and then forget to stop as they get older. You wouldn't do the same thing with a friend or a colleague or the rest of your family. Nevertheless, it's an easy trap to fall into, at least to some extent. Maybe it's quicker to do it yourself, or you can't see the need for everyone to know what's happening, or you think if they don't know about it they can't interfere – or say no.

If you don't share, however, other people don't have that feeling of all being in it together. Even if they don't need the information per se, they still need to be one of the group, and that means sharing information with them.

And not only information. If you're all part of the team, all on the same side, you'll need to share other things too. Knowledge, control, power, credit – sharing can be scary, but the risks of not sharing are higher.

Whether you're organising a family anniversary, or running a high-powered sales team, or organising a local campaign, you need to involve people in order to motivate them. They want a piece of the action too. They want to know where they fit into the bigger picture. They want to know that if they work hard they'll get a share in the credit. They want to feel they're making a difference. All of these things are only possible if you give them a share in everything you can. That way, you'll get a share of their hard work, goodwill and commitment in return.

> # YOU NEED TO INVOLVE PEOPLE
> # IN ORDER TO MOTIVATE THEM

Say thank you properly

We all like to be appreciated. Clichéd but true. Not only that, but people appreciate being appreciated, if you see what I mean, so the act of thanking them will make them want to do their best for you next time. After all, they can be pretty sure their efforts will be noticed and their contribution valued. So everyone wins, because you get what you need from them, and they get to feel good.

There's an art to thanking people. Although almost any thanks is better than none, there are many nuanced ways to say thank you, and finding the best one is a real skill.

The first thing is to get the proportion right. This isn't difficult once you think about it, but it's easy to get wrong if you blunder in thoughtlessly. You don't want to overthank or underthank, do you? You can patronise or embarrass people by making a huge deal out of a relatively minor contribution. By the same token, you don't want to undervalue someone's help by calling out a cursory 'Oh, thanks, by the way...' as you leave the room, if they've put in a huge amount of effort and given up loads of free time to you.

And what have they done? Before you say thank you, think this one through. Oh, all right, you don't need to analyse what you're thanking them for every time they make you a cup of tea – but when they've worked hard on a project, or helped organise your wedding, or listened to you moan for days on end, or spent hours researching stuff for you. You need to think it through so you can tell them.

This is at the heart of a really valuable thank you. Let the person know exactly what you are grateful for. Their endless patience? The evenings they gave up? Their attention to detail? Their kindness? Their calmness in a crisis? Say it to them in words – never assume they know. Yes, they know what they did, but they don't know what you valued unless you tell them. Say it or write it, but spell it out.

Now decide how you're going to say thanks. It's not just about what the person has done, but also who they are. Some people much prefer a private thank you. Some will appreciate a personal gift, others might like a card with a carefully worded message. Some will want public appreciation. Don't thoughtlessly give a bottle of wine to a teetotaller, or a bouquet of lilies to someone with hay fever, or throw a surprise party for someone who hates surprises.

An unexpected thank you is worth more than an obvious one. A note or a small gift or a special phone call to say thanks out of the blue are worth much more than the thank you that is accepted as standard, for example thanking the conductor at the end of the school concert. Which means – I hope you'll realise – that you really need to think hard if you're giving a routine thanks to some- one who has really earned it, if you want them to feel properly appreciated. It takes a lot to make it sound genuine when you have to say it anyway. The way to do that is to make it as specific and personal as possible, to show you've truly noticed what they've done.

> **THEY KNOW WHAT THEY DID, BUT THEY DON'T KNOW WHAT YOU VALUED UNLESS YOU TELL THEM**

RULE 69

Get under their skin

Alright, so appreciation is important for pretty much everyone. But what else motivates people? What else encourages them to do their best time and again? What makes it worth your colleague's while to cover when you're out of the office, or worth your friend's time to babysit for you, or worth your uncle's effort to teach you the basics of book-keeping for your freelance business, or worth your librarian remembering to put your favourite books under the counter for next time you're in?

Get under people's skin and understand what drives them – what motivates them. They're all different. Yes, that makes it tricky, but it makes it interesting too. Personally, I enjoy the challenge of figuring out how to make a particular person feel good. I have one colleague at the moment who can be tricky in meetings, but she's easy to handle so long as she feels important. That's what does it for her. It's not difficult, or untrue, to make reference to how crucial her input is, or what a difference it will make to have this task done thoroughly, and she's happy to oblige so long as she feels essential to things.

I know people who are motivated by money, of course, but it's the primary motivator for far fewer people than you might think. Some people want status – they'll do anything for a fancy job title. Or job satisfaction. Recognition is another very common one, which is related to appreciation but not quite the same thing – they need to know you've noticed, and often that other people have noticed too.

A fair number of people want responsibility more than anything else. In due course they'll probably want the money and status that might go with it, but they're not the key things. What they really want is to feel trusted with something that matters. They want to prove to you (and maybe to themselves) that they're up to being put in charge of something or someone bigger than before.

Most people have more than one motivator, although one will generally be stronger than the others. So often linked to responsibility, but definitely not the same thing, is challenge. Some people get bored unless you give them the chance to do something new or different or bigger or more difficult than before. If you want to keep them onside, let them get their teeth into something meaty.

I can think of a few people I've encountered over the years, at work and among friends, family and acquaintances, whose main motivating drive is freedom. They want to be given a destination and left alone to get there in their own way. (Come to think of it, I'm like that myself.) Autonomy is hugely important to them, whether they're functioning alone or running their own team, and they'll be happy to work with you so long as you back right off and leave them to it. Often they know what they're doing. If not, they can be tricky to handle but it can be done. Keep the project within their capabilities, or establish very clear parameters.

As you can see, it's not hard to motivate people once you've identified what gets them out of bed in the morning. Just give it some thought and you'll be halfway there already.

> # I ENJOY THE CHALLENGE OF FIGURING OUT HOW TO MAKE A PARTICULAR PERSON FEEL GOOD

Criticise constructively

It's not easy to keep people on board when you're criticising them, which means you have to be very careful how you do it so you don't lose their goodwill. Square one is being sure that you really need to do it at all. We all know people who are more critical than most. That's not because they're unlucky enough to be surrounded by people turning in far shoddier work than everyone else. It's because they look for faults they don't need to, or won't allow minor issues to pass without comment, or can only tolerate things being done their way, or are on some kind of power trip. As a Rules player, you certainly shouldn't be one of these people.

Consider the big picture before you criticise at all. There will certainly be times when it is wise to put people straight, and when they'll benefit from being shown a better way, but there are also times when it's far better to keep shtum. Even if the point is worth making, it might not be worth making right now. For example, you wouldn't give an actor criticism of their performance five minutes before they go on stage for their opening night. Maybe tomorrow, when they have time to absorb it before the next performance.

Which brings me to another point – it's futile offering criticism for something the other person can't change. Worse than futile in fact: it's counter-productive. So don't tell your actor friend they're too old for the role. Equally, don't tell someone about to give a big presentation later today that they need to write the thing again from scratch. It might have been good advice a month ago, but it's not helpful now. If they can't do anything about it, don't pass comment.

If you decide it would be productive to criticise someone, and now is a good time, you want to make your comments as helpful as possible, and avoid putting the other person's back up. If you make them feel bad about themselves, they're likely to resent you, and resent your comments. Not only will you risk losing their support, you also risk them not putting your advice into practice. In which case you've gained nothing at all, and are worse off than before you opened your mouth.

It's a good general rule to preface any negative comments with a positive one, and then to finish off with a positive remark too. So you might say, 'I think your basic business model is excellent. The financials could do with some more detail, especially the cash flow forecast...' Then finish up with another positive, 'You've obviously got a good handle on your customer profile'. Be as specific as you can, because otherwise it's not actually helpful. So explain what additional detail the financial plans need, and why.

None of us really likes being criticised, even though we want our presentation or our new business or our performance to be as good as possible. So the best approach is to make the positive points personal – you did this well, you're great at that – but be impersonal about the negative elements. That means instead of saying 'You need to speak louder', say 'It's not always easy to hear at the back'. Instead of 'Your report was badly presented', say 'It's worth spending time on the look of the report. It would look best in a single typeface...'. You want to leave the other person feeling you've given them some positive feedback plus some really helpful advice. Not as though they've been put through the mill.

> # IF THEY CAN'T DO ANYTHING ABOUT IT, DON'T PASS COMMENT

Agree without agreeing

I used to have arguments with my mother sometimes when I really didn't mean to. It would start because she would complain about someone or something, and I would defend them. For example, she might be irritated that she'd had to queue for 'hours' in the post office. I might think this was unfair because the people ahead of her in the queue could be elderly and need time and support. And I'd say so in what I thought was a chatty fashion. However, she would then argue with me in some way (they should have more staff, they should have a quick-service queue, she'd gone at what shouldn't have been a busy time, everyone in front of her had been young), and before I knew it, we'd be squabbling. I never quite knew how I'd got into an argument I didn't want, and getting back out of it always seemed tricky.

My mother was not the only person this ever happened with, of course, and I should have grasped what was going on much sooner. My attempt to put the opposite perspective always seemed fair and balanced to me, but to my mother it sounded like a criticism of her view. So it's really no surprise that she took issue with me when I did it.

Eventually I clicked that there was no way to present the opposite view without starting an argument. I just had to agree that 15 minutes was a tedious wait in the post office. Which I suppose it is. And in the case of the post office queue it was fairly simple just to shut up. But what about those times when I really disagreed with her? For example, she might moan about one of her neighbours behaving in a way I honestly thought was entirely reasonable.[17] I wasn't going to lie and say the neighbour was being difficult when I didn't think so.

---

[17] I don't want to suggest my mother did nothing but moan and complain. She could also be a lot of fun. Sometimes.

This was my problem – how to avoid being a hypocrite while simultaneously avoiding a row? I felt I was damned if I did and damned if I didn't. I couldn't bring myself to join in criticising an innocent neighbour, so how did I get out of that one?

I'll tell you how. And it goes back to the Rule about validating people's feelings. When called on to express an opinion, I didn't comment on the neighbour at all. I confined myself to commenting on my mother's emotional reaction: 'Yes, that would make you angry.' Well, being my mother it would anyway – obviously, because here she was, angry about it. Suddenly this meant I could agree with her with integrity, and avoid an argument. It didn't matter that it wouldn't make *me* angry, because we weren't talking about me.

I use this approach frequently now – whenever someone is upset about something and I don't share their viewpoint. Interestingly I've never been asked in one of these conversations – by my mother or anyone else what my personal view is. They're always wrapped up in their own emotions at these moments, and it doesn't cross their minds. They assume I'm agreeing with them. And I feel comfortable because actually I'm not.

> # THERE'S NO WAY TO PRESENT THE OPPOSITE VIEW WITHOUT STARTING AN ARGUMENT

RULE 72

Let them win

A big part of getting people on your side is negotiating. Whether you're agreeing a business deal, arranging with your siblings to share care of your elderly parents, asking your boss for a pay rise, agreeing bedtime with your child, or splitting the bill after a meal out with friends, you need to know how the other person is feeling and what will make them want to co-operate with you. And the good news is that almost everyone has the same basic criterion when they're negotiating.

Everyone wants to win. Simple, really. Let them come out on top and they'll be happy to agree the deal.

You'll have spotted a flaw in this approach. Yep – if they win, where does that leave you? Well, that's the interesting bit. If you play your cards right, you can win too. And that should be your aim in any negotiation. In fact, it's the only outcome that can possibly work.

Think of a simple business deal. Let's say a market trader selling to a customer. As it's a market stall, the customer isn't going to pay the asking price. They're going to haggle. So it's become a negotiation, albeit of the most basic kind. You've been in this situation yourself I'm sure, and what generally happens is that you agree a price somewhere in the middle. So who's won? Well, you have of course. You've got the item at a price you consider worth it – if you hadn't, you'd have walked away. But hang on, the stallholder didn't have to accept your offer. They could have refused to sell you the thing. So they must be feeling like a winner too, if they agreed to the deal.

And that's what you're after. As you may know, this is known as a win/win deal. And it doesn't only apply to business deals and money transactions. It applies to any agreement you're trying to reach, with your friends, colleagues, family, kids, neighbours.

Let's go back to your kids' bedtime. You could just tell them it's 8pm and you don't want to hear any argument. However, as they get older, you're likely to want to allow them some input, without allowing them free rein over when they go to bed. It's good for them to start learning to regulate their own timetable. Then again, you don't want it to turn into a row followed by a long sulk, or a rebellion, when they feel you've won the argument and they've lost it. Look, they know you're not going to let them go to bed at 2am. They're expecting some kind of limit, broadly in line with where you've drawn the line when they were younger. Which means it really should be possible to strike a deal where you both feel you've got what you want – so that should be your aim.

The next few Rules will help you fine-tune your negotiating antennae so you can turn all your deals into win/win ones. Yes, even when you're negotiating with your kids. Understand what they're looking for and how they think, and it becomes much easier to work with, not against, each other.

> # EVERYONE WANTS TO WIN.
> # SIMPLE, REALLY

Make it three-dimensional

I mentioned in the last Rule that haggling over a market stall purchase is the simplest kind of negotiation. That's because the only thing up for discussion is the price. You could almost argue that this doesn't constitute a negotiation at all because there's only one moving piece – the price. To negotiate properly, you need more moving pieces. You might call them variables.

In a business deal, you might be trying to agree not only on the price, but also on the quality, the delivery times, the degree of finish, the after-sales care, the warranty – there are lots of moving pieces. Any and all of them can change, until you arrive at a point where everyone is happy. For example, you might agree to sell at a lower price so long as you have longer to deliver, or they do their own packaging.

You can do the same thing with any kind of deal, if you can find the right variables. And you can introduce ones the other person hasn't even thought of: 'Would you stay on as Chair of the committee for another year if we brought in a co-chair to share the workload? Or if we changed the day of our monthly meetings to a Wednesday to fit round your other commitments?'

When it comes to your children's bedtime, you can introduce any moving pieces you like. If they don't like the deal they don't have to agree, but it's more likely they'll get the hang of it themselves and start suggesting their own variables. So you could make bedtime slightly later at weekends than during the school week, or later if their homework is up to date, or if they don't spend any additional time on their computers as a result, or on days when their bedroom is tidy, or if they earn it by doing chores – it's entirely up to you. If they want to leave their bedroom messy and keep bedtime where it is, fine. Chances are that they'll be happy to negotiate though.

Variables are the key to a successful deal, because they provide opportunities for lots of little wins. Plenty of chances for the other person to feel they've come out on top – while leaving lots of other little victories for you. Now all you have to do is work out which victories are most important to *them,* and which ones *you* really need to clinch. Of course, each of these is a moving piece, and can have its own point of balance where you can both win. Your kids feel like winners because they get to go to bed half an hour later, but you've won because now they'll be doing the washing up every evening after you've eaten.

There really is no limit to what you can bring into a negotiation in order to fill out all these variable factors and give yourself plenty to negotiate with. You can be as creative as you like about what you suggest. The other person can always say no.

> # WORK OUT WHICH VICTORIES ARE MOST IMPORTANT TO *THEM*, AND WHICH ONES *YOU* REALLY NEED TO CLINCH

RULE 74

Give and take

Now you have all your variable, movable pieces, you'd better start moving them. This is where the real bargaining comes in. And there's one principle you need to bear in mind at all times: never give without taking. It's a process of constant trade-off. If your client asks for a better price, say that could be possible if you had a longer lead time, or if they paid up front, or you delivered to one central point and they handled the distribution out to their branches.

Remember, the other person has got to feel as if they're winning before they'll say yes. So the corollary of this is that you shouldn't expect to take without also giving. Indeed, you shouldn't want to. You want the other person to feel as good as possible about the whole deal so they won't just walk away from it. And so they'll be happy to deal with you in the future. So offer faster delivery if they'll pay up front, or suggest you could lower the price if they lower the spec.

This sense of balance is a vital theme that runs through all negotiations. It's important that you give, but not so much that you seem to be a pushover. That's not a reputation you want. You want this person – and anyone they speak to – to know that there's no point making unreasonable demands of you because you're not going to fall for it. However, you're pleasant and realistic, and positive to do business with if you're treated fairly.

So whatever they ask, never say 'Yes'. Always say 'Yes, if…'. When your brother asks if you'll take your elderly father to all his medical appointments, don't just say yes. Say yes, you could do that if he'll take responsibility for Dad's household admin. If your colleague wants you to write their presentation for them because that's one of your strengths, you might say yes, if they'll keep an eye on your accounts when you're on holiday next month.

It's worth pointing out here that not all negotiations declare themselves as such. If you have a big business meeting to discuss the terms of a new contract, you know that's a negotiation and you can switch into gear. When your child asks to move their bedtime, or your brother asks your to manage your dad's medical visits, it isn't always immediately obvious that you're in a negotiation. But you probably are.

The only time this isn't the case is when you're genuinely happy to do something for nothing. That's fine – I hope we all do people favours without expecting anything in return. I'm not suggesting we should always be asking what's in it for us. It's important to be generous. But no one wants to be a sucker. Your elderly neighbour might really need you to help with her weekly shop, and it's a kindness to do it for her without expecting anything in return. But your colleague could perfectly well write his own presentation, so it's quite reasonable to suggest you swap favours.

> ## IT'S IMPORTANT TO BE GENEROUS. BUT NO ONE WANTS TO BE A SUCKER

RULE 75

Know what you both want

I hope you wouldn't go into any negotiation without knowing what your bottom line is. You can't turn a profit on this deal if the price drops below a certain level, or there's no way your kids are going to bed later than 9pm, or you have two evenings a week to give to the football club and that's it. You can't be confident you'll come out of the discussion successfully unless you know what constitutes success.

I knew a small publisher who was tremendously excited when a big supermarket chain wanted to buy several thousand copies of one of her books. They started negotiating a price, and she just couldn't get them to pay what she'd calculated she needed to make the deal viable. In the end she walked away from it. Lots of people thought she was mad, but she was absolutely right. It could have bankrupted her. If she hadn't been clear what her bottom line was, she might have made a huge mistake and said yes.

Knowing your own bottom line is sometimes the easy bit. It just takes intelligent thought before you start negotiating, and an awareness of how the pieces fit together (you might be able to accept a lower price, for example, if you secured payment up front). However, the other person also has a bottom line, and you need to know that too.

Look, if the other person doesn't reach their bottom line, they'll walk away. And that's not what you want. You need to make this deal work for them too. So don't make demands they can't possibly agree to, or screw them down on price until it's not worth their while to sign the deal, or ask them to give up more time than they have. You'll lose their goodwill and you'll lose the deal. And you risk parting with a measure of ill feeling or resentment that isn't going to help any future dealings you might have.

It generally becomes clear over the course of discussions what the other person's bottom line is. However, more often than not, the best way to establish it is through the blindingly simple ploy of asking them, 'What's your bottom line?'. Of course, you can't assume they'll give you a straight answer (this is a negotiation after all), but their answer will still give you a big clue. If there's enough trust between you, or the circumstances are right, you might well feel the answer is honest. For example, if you're trying to agree terms with someone to become treasurer of your society, they'll probably give you a genuine response when you ask how much time they can give.

And it's not only their bottom line that matters. Sometimes there are concessions – perhaps minor ones to you – that will be important to them. These might be significant, such as the terms for payment, but they might be quite quirky. For example, some people might agree to more than you would expect in exchange for a photo of them with the star of your football team, or the promise of a tour of your factory in some exotic location, or the chance to look good in front of their MD, or a pair of those Spiderman pyjamas they've been wanting.

> **YOU CAN'T BE CONFIDENT YOU'LL COME OUT OF THE DISCUSSION SUCCESSFULLY UNLESS YOU KNOW WHAT CONSTITUTES SUCCESS**

RULE 76

Get all their cards on the table

You can think of your variables, your moving pieces, as being moved back and forth on a set of old-fashioned scales until everything is in balance. If one moves across to this side, another one has to move that way to compensate. In a sense, these are everyone's wants and desires being balanced against each other until everyone is satisfied that the deal is fair. Bit like the scales of justice.

Once everything is perfectly positioned, you can shake hands, sign on the dotted line, and it's a done deal. But you do have to be sure that all the movable pieces stay flexible before you sign off on the deal.

If you agree a firm price in exchange for an extended deadline, before you've completed discussions, you've glued down those two weights in your scales. So when they ask for something else, you can no longer say 'Yes, but it will cost you . . .', because you've confirmed the price. That was silly of you, wasn't it? So don't agree anything firmly until you've got the whole deal in place. Just say, 'That price could be possible. Let's put it on one side for the moment while we discuss delivery.'

And here's another thing to look out for. Suppose you reach an agreement, shake on it, and then your client says, 'By the way, we'd like to extend our payment time from thirty days to sixty.' Or your child says, 'Now we've sorted out bedtime, can I also have my phone in my room? All my friends are allowed to . . .'.[18]

---

[18] I remember back when I was a teenager, it was *de rigueur* even then to finish every request to parents with 'all my friends are allowed to'. It had to be delivered with just the right blend of pleading and petulance.

Dammit! You could have made that one of the moving pieces, only you've gone and agreed the deal already. You have nothing left to trade with because you've used up all the variables that matter.

People can be slippery, especially when they want something they're not sure they're going to get. And any canny negotiator knows that it can be a good idea to keep something up their sleeve. You can't ask them to make any more concessions now, because you've agreed the terms, so you have no bargaining chips left. You either agree to their extended payment time – or whatever – or you lose the whole deal. They are well aware of this, however disingenuously they might make out that this is a whole separate matter. Of course it isn't. It's just an issue they didn't want to bring into the main negotiation because they didn't want to have to give any ground on it.

The way to prevent this is to ask, before you fix the deal in stone, whether there's anything else they want to discuss, include, alter, agree, rearrange. If they say no, they're on the back foot if they try to introduce it later because you can say, 'No, we agreed there weren't any other points to cover. That's the deal as it stands.' They really can't argue with that so long as you've made it quite clear. And if they ever negotiate with you again, they'll know not to try it on with you.

> **PEOPLE CAN BE SLIPPERY, ESPECIALLY WHEN THEY WANT SOMETHING THEY'RE NOT SURE THEY'RE GOING TO GET**

Give them a get-out

When you negotiate, the whole exercise doesn't only happen on paper. It also matters how the other person is feeling. No one likes to lose face. It's not a nice feeling. So sometimes people can dig their heels in simply because of how they feel, regardless of whether the deal on the table is workable. You have to look after their feelings if you want to come out of this with a good deal and your positive relationship intact.

This is where your win/win approach is so strong. However, there may be times when they need persuading that they've won. Or when winning a particular part of the deal matters to them as much as winning the overall negotiation. So you need to be on the lookout to make sure they don't lose face. Otherwise they may be tempted to give up on the deal either because they're embarrassed to concede a particular point, or even just to spite you.

This is a good example of the point a couple of Rules back about making sure you know what the other person wants. That will help you identify these potential sticking points. If you can, of course, you'll give ground on these in exchange for concessions that matter to you. Sometimes, however, that's not practicable.

Suppose your child wants a 9.30pm bedtime. That's when *all* her friends go to bed.[19] You are adamant that you won't go beyond 9pm. It might well be that deep down she doesn't really mind going to bed at 9pm. What she minds is having to tell her friends that she has to go to bed earlier than they do. (No, I don't know why she believes them either. I guess because she wants to.) So you need to find her something she is happy to tell them, if you want to get her to agree to 9pm. You want to find her a 'but' she can tell her friends: 'I have to go to bed at nine, *but* ...'. OK, the sky's your limit here. You could say 9pm *but* we'll make it 10.30pm

---

[19] Apparently.

in the holidays. Or you could find something completely unre-
lated – 9pm, *but* you can have a bedroom makeover, or 9pm *but*
you can have a raise in pocket money too, or 9pm *but* every time
you go to bed on time without fuss all week, you can have extra
time online on Saturday.

Same with your business deal. The other person promised the
boss they'd get a particular price out of you, but in fact it's just not
realistic. You couldn't sign the deal at that price. So you might say,
'I can't quite get down to that price *but* I can extend your payment
terms.' You've given them something they can go back to the boss
with which means they won't lose face. You've given them an
escape route, so they feel like a success and not a failure.

> # YOU HAVE TO LOOK AFTER THEIR FEELINGS IF YOU WANT TO COME OUT OF THIS WITH A GOOD DEAL

Never be scared

The psychology of negotiating is hugely important, and the bigger and more important the deal, the more the other person is likely to be trying every trick in the book to get what they want from you. And that means they'll be on the lookout for any apparent weakness – contractual, practical, financial or psychological. I should just point out that when I say 'the bigger and more important the deal', I mean to them. This might be an everyday deal to you, but it could mean the future of their small business. Or you might be happy with the status quo regarding bedtimes, but your child cares desperately.

Conversely, reaching an agreement might be more crucial to you than it is to them. Listen, you can't assume everyone else under-stands the importance of win/win as clearly as you do. Even if they do, it might not matter as much to them. Suppose you're one tiny supplier to the huge multinational you're negotiating with. They don't need you half as much as you need them, so why would they care whether you come out feeling good? They're up for a deal that works for them, but they're not going to cry into their pillows if they have to go and find another supplier instead. You can't count on them to be looking for a win/win deal.

OK, take your child's bedtime. She doesn't care how you feel, except in as much as it will get her what she wants. She knows you'll always love her no matter what. So although you have the authority to impose the rules you want, she can make you feel horrible about it. She can shout and rant, or sulk, or emotionally blackmail – if she's a normal child, I'm sure she's adept at all of these when she feels her back's against the wall – so you'll feel bludgeoned into making concessions unless you're extremely strong-willed.

In all these scenarios, the other person has the potential to walk off (or storm off) and leave you feeling worse about it than they do. Not reaching an agreement might be their Plan B, but it's your Plan Z.

The one thing you must never, ever do is let them see that you're scared, worried, anxious, nervous about not finding any centre ground. If they can see they've got you on the run, that no deal would be worse for you than any deal, they've got you over a barrel and I can't help you. No one can. They can demand anything they like and threaten to walk away if you don't agree, and you'll have to say yes or give into a deal that really doesn't work.

There are always going to be times when you need agreement badly, and are worried about what will happen if you don't reach it. You can't always avoid the situation. What you can do is maintain a calm and unflustered front, and appear keen to strike a deal but prepared to walk away if you have to. You know it's not true, I know it's not true, but for goodness' sake, don't let them know it's not true.

> IF THEY CAN SEE THEY'VE GOT YOU ON THE RUN, THAT NO DEAL WOULD BE WORSE FOR YOU THAN ANY DEAL, THEY'VE GOT YOU OVER A BARREL

Don't get caught on the hop

Wouldn't it be great if everyone dealt fairly with everyone else all the time? But most people, some of the time (including you and me), want or need a thing badly enough that they put their own interests ahead of other people's. It's human nature. And sometimes they want something badly enough to be quite underhand about it.

One of the classic ways to get you to agree to something when you don't mean to is to put you on the spot. Unscrupulous companies play a questionable version of this game when they offer you a fantastic deal on their holiday or car or timeshare, but tell you the deal is only on the table for a few hours so you'll have to sign on the dotted line now if you want the best deal.

Most decent people would baulk at doing this to you face to face, but they'll still exploit the potential of putting you under time pressure. This is a classic negotiating technique, and it can be easy to get caught up in it before you realise that it's just a ruse.

When the discussion is more ad hoc, this is an easy trick. Your daughter might try to discuss her bedtime when your mind is elsewhere, or when you're hurrying to go out, in the hope you won't think the issue through properly and will agree anyway.

It's also one of the arguments against putting 'any other business' on the agenda for meetings – some people will raise a contentious subject without warning under AOB, when no one else has time to prepare their case, in the hope of getting agreement. By that time in a meeting everyone is generally more than ready to get away, and agreeing is generally faster than arguing. At least that's what the perpetrator is hoping.

So be on your guard against this kind of ploy. Not only can you be sucked into agreeing something you didn't really mean to, but you'll also unwittingly encourage the other person to try the same trick with you again in future, now they've discovered you're a sucker for it.

You don't have to tell the other person you're on to them, mind you. They won't like being caught out, and you don't want to get on the wrong side of them. You can just let them know that now isn't a good time, or suggest that this item warrants a full discussion and should go on the agenda for the next meeting so everyone has time to prepare for it.

In fact if anyone tries to put you on the spot with a request, and claims it's urgent (especially when it's more urgent to them than to you), I'd recommend the response a good friend of mine always used to use. It works on colleagues, friends, family and even on your kids. In fact, it's brilliant for kids. If anyone pressed this friend for a decision when he didn't have time to deal with it he'd always say, 'If you need an answer now, it's no.'

> ## YOU DON'T HAVE TO TELL THE OTHER PERSON YOU'RE ON TO THEM

DIFFICULT
PEOPLE

Anyone can be difficult to handle in the wrong situation, but some people seem to manage it a great deal of the time. Whether they're typically aggressive, negative, whinging or controlling, they present particular challenges. Coping with them – let alone getting the best out of them – is a constant frustration.

The good news is that if you know how to adapt your own behaviour, you can improve your relationship with almost anyone. They may still be tricky, but you'll be able to take them along with you once you've learned the secrets, strategies and ploys for getting past the barriers they put in your way.

Not only that, but once you've mastered rubbing along with these people, many of them will begin to see you as an ally, and it will be increasingly easy to get their co-operation. So this section is all about learning to manage the difficult people in your life.

RULE 80

There's only one person you can change

Some difficult people really aren't your problem. You encounter them occasionally, or maybe they aren't difficult that often. Others might be tricky a lot of the time, and they might be your boss or your father or your own child. Not so easy to avoid.

The following Rules cover a variety of types of difficult people. Simply understanding the person can help. And there are some strategies you can use to make encounters with them easier. But you must recognise one key thing – you can't change other people, as we saw in Rule 12. They will still be difficult in the situations that push their buttons. You might, if everything goes well, eventually train them to behave differently around you. For example, an emotional blackmailer might learn in time that their tactics are wasted on you, and stop bothering. But you cannot stop them being an emotional blackmailer underneath, and towards other people. Only they can do that.

This even applies, incidentally, to your own child. There's as much nature as nurture there,[20] and a history you can't alter. You can show them that their behaviour doesn't work but, in the end, they're the only one who can change it.

So, working this through logically, there's only one person who you can change, and that's yourself. If someone else's behaviour makes you feel yucky, stressed, irritated, frustrated, upset – it's your job, not theirs, to do something about it. Your reaction is your stuff.

Don't tell me I'm being harsh because I'm not. I'm just stating a fact. Like it or not, and however much the other person isn't helping, if you want to feel differently, it's down to you to do something

---

[20] Maybe more – don't ask me, I'm not a scientist.

about it. It's not easy – of course it isn't, or you'd have done it already. But the first step to coping with difficult people is to grasp that if you don't like the way you feel, change it.

And in answer to your next question, no, I can't tell you how. They're your feelings and I can't change them. Got it? My advice is to start with a variation on one of the following and take it from there. Really, anything that works for you (and doesn't harm anyone else) is good. So here are a few initial suggestions of things that help some people:

- Stop listening (not always an option but sometimes it helps – probably best to still look like you're listening).

- Visualise the words going over your head.

- Think about how much worse it must be for the other person – I mean, would you like to feel constantly angry, or negative, or out of control?

- Practise responding constructively. If you can manage the interaction effectively, you'll feel much better than if you can't.

YOUR REACTION IS YOUR STUFF

It's scary being controlled

Some people's behaviour is, frankly, atrocious. I mean, most people behave pretty well most of the time, but there are some people who just don't get it. They're sullen and rude, or drunk half the time, or never listen to what you say, or are wholly unreliable. So why?

I can't speak for every person I've never met, but in my experience most people whose behaviour is extreme in an undesirable fashion isn't really in control. After all, why would anyone choose to alienate, offend, upset, disgust, deter other people if it was up to them? Sadly, it may not be up to them.

All of us aim to be in control of our own selves, and it's frankly terrifying if you aren't. Yet this is the case for very many people for one reason or another – whether all the time or only sometimes.

So why can't these people help the way they behave? Who is controlling them if they're not? Well, there are lots of possible culprits. Alcohol, prescription drugs, recreational drugs, gambling, compulsive shopping – these can all be addictions, can all take over someone's life. Addiction is, by definition, not a choice. Maybe these people are driven by something that happened in their childhood, maybe they once made an unwise choice in the past, maybe they have mental health issues tangled up in there somewhere – or maybe not. It doesn't matter. They are now in a world in which the addiction is pulling the strings. And that's very scary for them, but they're trapped and they don't know how to get out.

And there are other things than addiction which can control people. Mental health problems, from bipolar disorder to OCD, can affect their behaviour in ways they can do nothing about.

Imagine trying to cope with an autistic spectrum disorder, or Tourette's, or schizophrenia, among people who have no experience of it and don't understand why you behave as you do. Would you explain to everyone why you were behaving oddly (if you even realised it yourself), knowing the stigma that some people attach to mental illness?

So maybe, maybe those badly behaved people aren't just rude or boorish or freaky. Maybe they're scared and out of control – at least in some aspects of their lives – and trying desperately to cope with an impossible situation that isn't of their making.

I'm not qualified to diagnose anyone, but I find that when I encounter someone tricky it helps to consider what unconscious demons are getting in their way. It doesn't matter whether I'm right – whether they actually have them. As soon as I perceive them as someone with ADHD, or Asperger's, or alcoholism, or indeed any kind of addiction or disorder, I find it far easier to put up with their difficult behaviour, and much easier to be kind to them. If I'm anywhere near the mark, it's the least I can do for them. And if I'm wrong and they're just a nasty piece of work – well, it still makes interactions smoother, and I get to feel virtuous.

> # THEY'RE TRAPPED AND THEY DON'T KNOW HOW TO GET OUT

If they feel small, they'll big themselves up

This is how almost all bullies work. They belittle other people and do their best to turn them into victims. Why? Because a victim is submissive to their aggressor – or, to put it another way, the aggressor is dominant. Bigger, more powerful, more in control. This is the feeling that the bully wants. And why do they want it? Because deep down inside, they feel powerless. Maybe someone else is dominating them, maybe their life feels out of their control, maybe they're secretly scared.

Not only can they feel bigger by making someone else feel smaller, often they also gain (or feel they gain) the respect and admiration of their acolytes – who in fact often surround them in an attempt to avoid being bullied themselves.

People are complicated things. Of course, nothing justifies bullying. But you can sympathise with the reasons behind it without having to condone the bully's way of dealing with them. And although it doesn't make it all alright if you are on the receiving end – or someone you love is – it often helps if you understand where the bully is coming from. And it can help you feel less intimidated if you can see the bully as they see themselves: weak, powerless, victimised.

Obviously this realisation doesn't stop the bullying, it doesn't make everything OK, it doesn't mean the problem goes away. But it can make it a bit less unbearable, knowing that the process isn't even making the bully happy – it's just a symptom of their general unhappiness.

I've encountered a lot of bullies over the years, but I can't recall a truly happy one. The really happy, confident, self-assured, relaxed people I know never bully anyone. Why would they need to? There'd be nothing in it for them.

Sometimes, understanding why someone bullies can be what it takes to resolve things. It's very hard for the person on the receiving end to do this, although not impossible. However, good schools have a high success rate, and a good manager or parent can often sort out such problems in their team or their family. The key is to listen to the bully, find out what is making them feel powerless, and help resolve it. It seems counter-intuitive to help someone who is behaving so badly, but if it makes things better for everyone, it has to make sense. Besides, the bullies often really need help, and we mustn't be blinded by our anger or hurt at their badly chosen approach to helping themselves. No one thinks, 'I'm going to try bullying people – that might make me feel better'. It's an instinctive thing they haven't thought through, and most bullies don't recognise that description of themselves. Obviously – because they see themselves as powerless and victimised, and that's not their idea of a bully.

> # I'VE ENCOUNTERED A LOT OF BULLIES OVER THE YEARS, BUT I CAN'T RECALL A TRULY HAPPY ONE

Shouty people want to be heard

Think about it. I don't know if you're the type who almost never gets riled, or the type who likes to let off steam several times a week. But either way, what is it that makes you raise your voice at someone? Or let's put it another way – why does your instinct tell you that speaking softly isn't going to get the result you want?

I'll bet that almost every time, it's because you feel the other person won't hear you unless you shout. I don't necessarily mean that literally. I mean they won't fully take on board what you're saying unless you force them to listen by making it impossible for them not to. I'm not here to judge whether you're right, or whether you're justified (not least because I'm not above shouting myself occasionally, although I usually regret it afterwards – not always, but usually).

So now turn it around and think about when other people shout at you. It's not very nice being shouted at, and when it happens to me I generally want to make it stop as quickly as possible. And the way to make that happen is to listen, and to show that you're listening. That's what the shouty person wants, so it stands to reason that the way to make them stop shouting is to give it to them.

Suppose you're taking something faulty back to the shop you bought it from. The shop assistant doesn't grasp the problem, doesn't acknowledge that it needs fixing, doesn't recognise their responsibility to fix it or replace it. They are going through stock replies which aren't relevant, and they're clearly not listening. Feel like shouting? Of course you do.[21]

---

[21] Although being a Rules player you'll resist the temptation.

Now repeat the scenario in your head, but this time the shop assistant is listening closely to what you're saying, and asking intelligent, relevant questions. Still feel like shouting? No, of course not. You don't need to – they've clearly listened and you're getting what you need without having to shout.

Shouty people are frustrated people who feel they're not being heard. It's a good rule of thumb that any time someone raises their voice to you, they think you're not listening. If they're right, it's a clue that you need to hear them out fully. If they're wrong, and you really are listening, it's still a reliable gauge that you need to show you are. You know – don't interrupt them, repeat back the main points they're making, nod, show you've grasped their emotion as well as their words.

It follows from this, incidentally, that some people get shouted at more than others. Good listeners – who show they're listening – don't get shouted at nearly so often as people who interrupt, jump to conclusions, plough their own path regardless of what other people say, and are closed to other people. Which is fair enough, really.

IT'S A GOOD RULE OF THUMB
THAT ANY TIME SOMEONE
RAISES THEIR VOICE TO YOU,
THEY THINK YOU'RE NOT
LISTENING

Negative people can't half be useful

I always used to find negative people irritating. I'm not that way inclined myself – more likely to be the fool that rushes in, than to look for reasons not to do something. To me, negative people were pessimistic, depressing, disruptive and destructive. Couldn't see the point of them.

Then I worked in an organisation which relied on constantly bringing new products to market. We needed a steady flow of ideas. The ones that worked could make the company good money, but the ones that didn't grab our customers' imaginations made a loss – as well as using up time and resources that could otherwise have gone into a winning idea.

We had a director in our creative think tank who always looked on the negative side of any idea. Outside work he was a lovely guy with an unexpectedly positive approach to life. But in meetings he was always starting sentences with, 'It won't work, because . . .'. It drove me mad the way he could put the dampeners on almost any idea. Until I started to notice something.

Every time we ploughed ahead regardless of his concerns, we ended up with a product that just didn't sell well. Whereas when we managed to counter all his criticisms effectively, often adapting the original idea in order to do so, we generally managed to produce a really successful product. Actually, this guy may have sounded negative but he was being incredibly useful to us. The rest of us had a bit of a tendency to be enthusiastic about almost any idea, whereas he really took some persuading. And that meant our ideas were much better tested and honed before we gave them the green light.

I still find negativity irritating at times, but I recognise that it's an essential part of any project, from developing products to buying a house, packing for a holiday, starting a new business, planning a garden, changing jobs. You need someone to help you spot the problems before they happen, and that person is going to have to sound pretty negative at times if they're going to be of real help.

The other thing they'll need in order to help properly is to be specific. Negative people who just say, 'I bet it won't work', or 'You're wasting your time', without giving you a reason aren't helpful at all. Even if they turn out to be right. *Especially* if they turn out to be right. Because I bet if that happens, they'll be the first to say, 'I told you so', when actually they didn't really tell you so. They didn't tell you how or why you'd fail. They didn't tell you what precautions to take or which part of the project was flawed.

When you encounter a negative voice, always ask for specifics. 'Why won't it work? Which bit is the problem? What would you do differently?' If they won't give you any more detailed feedback, you have my permission[22] to ignore them and find them irritating. But if they can give you a reason for being negative, I really recommend you listen. Even if they're wrong, thinking the idea or project through with a sceptical eye can only help you get it right in the end.

> # YOU NEED SOMEONE TO HELP YOU SPOT THE PROBLEMS BEFORE THEY HAPPEN

---

[22] Which I hope you realise is worthless.

Control freaks know they're right

There are two kind of control freaks. First of all, there are the people who are always writing lists and never seem to run out of milk or forget to take their camera on holiday. Occasionally they can be a bit irksome, for example when they want you to settle arrangements with them way before you wanted to start thinking about it, but they're basically benign creatures who keep their control freakiness to themselves.

And then there's the other kind. The ones who want to control your life in some way. They're always telling you they know best, or expecting you to fit round them, or demanding that you behave in the way they would. These are the difficult ones. And when you don't fall in with their wishes, they can become tricky, even bullying or emotionally blackmailing to get what they want.

So what's behind their need to control you? Generally, control freaks are trying to compensate for a lack of control over their own lives. This might be something they feel now, or it might date back to an earlier time in their life when they felt out of control. Either way, they're trying to put it right now by doing their best to maintain control of everything they can. Possibly including you – because only then do they feel safe. They don't trust anyone else but themselves (perhaps from bitter experience) to make sure everything happens as they think it should. On some level they probably deserve your sympathy, but they won't thank you for it and, in the end, you can't solve their problems for them. Obviously.

I don't know many control freaks of this second kind who would describe themselves as such. In their view, they're right and you need to listen to them. They're doing it for you. Sometimes they genuinely care about you and can't bear the thought of you making a mistake and feeling powerless, so they're trying to protect you from yourself. Of course, if they're successful they're still making you powerless, because they've taken your control away from you themselves. But don't expect them to recognise that.

This kind of control freak is instinctively drawn to people who have low self-esteem, because such people are much more likely to accept the controller's authority. And the key to coping with control freaks is not to try to be pushy or aggressive or controlling or defensive back, but simply to be assertive and not accept their demands. Just tell them that you appreciate their advice and now you're going to make your own decision. Or let them know that you recognise your approach is different from theirs, but you don't consider either to be better or worse. So you'll carry on doing things your way, thank you.

The only person who can unmake a control freak is themselves. So there's no point imagining you can stop them doing it, and battling them will just make you stressed. The worst scenario is if you find yourself in a relationship with a control freak. You will need to learn to be very assertive and, if you really struggle, it's unlikely the relationship will survive unless your partner recognises how destructive their behaviour is – even when they truly believe they're doing everything for the best.

> # THE ONLY PERSON WHO CAN UNMAKE A CONTROL FREAK IS THEMSELVES

Blackmailers want to control you

Are you prone to feeling guilty? Or just to feeling there are some things you 'ought' to do? If so, you're easy prey for emotional blackmailers. These people are especially tricky to handle because they can manipulate your emotions and leave you with a Hobson's choice between doing something you don't want to, or feeling bad about not doing it. The only person who can come out of this the winner is the other person – if you capitulate.

I've known some otherwise lovely people who were prone to emotional blackmail. That makes it harder in fact – you care about them and want them to be happy. Which makes it more likely you'll give in to them. Listen, people who use emotional blackmail are genuinely needy – just not for the things they're trying to pressure you into doing. They often feel insecure or out of control, or they feel such a strong need for love or commitment from you that they'll try to force you to display it. Which really doesn't count, but somewhere in their mind it's better than risking its total absence.

They are trying to control you in order to get what they want. That's the bottom line. It might be a work colleague trying to get you to complete a report for them, or it might be your partner trying to make you stay with them by threatening suicide if you leave. In other words, the request – and your investment in the relationship – can be big or small.

I've known several parents who use emotional blackmail towards their children – 'I worked so hard to cook your dinner, I'll be sad if you don't eat it all up.' If you want your child to finish their food, either explain why it's sensible, or tell them that if they don't there'll be some kind of sanction. Or give them less of it. Or don't make them finish it. All those options are fine – emotional blackmail is not. Many parents keep it going long after their children have left home – 'You will visit, won't you? It's so lonely when no one calls round.'

Emotional blackmailers are trying to make *you* take responsibility for *their* emotional well-being. And they're trying to do it by taking over your emotions in some kind of warped swap. But of course the only emotions they're really interested in are your sense of fear or guilt – or at least of obligation. These are the weapons they use to control you.

If you are in any way susceptible to this – and just about everyone is at least sometimes, or with some people – you need to understand that the more these people are successful in their blackmailing, the harder they will find it to stop, or to take control of their own emotions. So by giving in, you may be providing their short-term need, but you're helping to perpetuate their long-term problem.[23]

Have the courage to say no. You can say it kindly but be firm. You can even say, 'Are you emotionally blackmailing me?'. That often makes them back off. If you are in a family relationship with an emotional blackmailer who seriously threatens you, you may need to remove yourself completely. The most important thing, regardless of the severity of the situation, is for you to recognise that you are being blackmailed and put boundaries around yourself. Refuse to take responsibility for other people's emotional well-being. Paradoxically, by forcing them to take responsibility for it, you'll be helping their emotional health. (But you won't be responsible for it.)

> # EMOTIONAL BLACKMAILERS ARE TRYING TO MAKE *YOU* TAKE RESPONSIBILITY FOR *THEIR* EMOTIONAL WELL-BEING

---

[23] Sorry – didn't mean that to come across as me emotionally blackmailing you.

RULE 87

Insecurity can cause mistrust

I know a woman who suffers from very low self-esteem. This affects all her relationships because she doesn't believe she's good enough for her partner. Why would he want to stay with her? What could he see in her? Surely he'll realise soon that she's not worth the effort, and he'll go off with someone else. What if he's already started to do that...? Was he really working late last week? You can see how her insecurity and fear of losing her partner leads easily on to becoming jealous and possessive.

This is sad enough, but what happens next is sadder in my view: she becomes so jealous that he can't stand it any longer, and he goes off with someone else. Her self-fulfilling prophecy has just reinforced her belief that she's not good enough and any partner is bound to leave her in the end.

It's easy to feel sympathy for her. But now look at it from her partner's perspective. He started off devoted and loyal, and she was so possessive, and mistrustful, and accused him of flirting or cheating endlessly, that in the end he decided he'd be better off out of the relationship.

It's no fun living with a jealous partner. Indeed, jealous friends and siblings and family and colleagues can be pretty stifling too. There is a difference between jealousy and envy. You might be envious of what others have, but jealousy is much more painful – it is the terrible fear of losing someone (or something you have) to another person. It generally has a lot to do with insecurity and low self-esteem.

So someone may be envious of what they perceive as your perfect relationship, or beautiful house, or career success, because they fear they will never have it themselves. Maybe because they don't think they deserve it.

But some friendships are beset by one person's jealousy that the other will find a 'better' friend soon and abandon them. This can be a huge problem in friendship groups, especially three-person ones, where one friend is convinced the other two are closer to each other. Some people can become very manipulative to prevent this happening, even though it might never have been a real threat.

You can help a jealous person by not antagonising them, and by avoiding behaviour that will rile them. But only up to a point. A partner whose experience has made them jealous may be mollified if you avoid flirting with other people or staying out all night without warning. However, if they start insisting on this, if they try to control your behaviour, you need to draw a line. This is *their* stuff and, while you can take care not to provoke it, the answer lies in them and not you. In the end, they have to learn to trust you or the relationship is doomed.

Your jealous friend needs reassurance, but also needs to understand that manipulative behaviour is the one thing that actually *will* push you away – the thing they fear. Your jealous sibling or colleague doesn't need to hear about your new job/car/house/clothes, so don't rub their nose in it. In the end though, if they have self-esteem they'll stop needing the trappings of success.

> # IF THEY HAVE SELF-ESTEEM, THEY'LL STOP NEEDING THE TRAPPINGS OF SUCCESS

RULE 88

Prejudice comes from ignorance

Almost all of us are potential targets of prejudice. Whether you're black, gay, Jewish, female, a single parent, Muslim, poorly educated, have a strong regional accent, or have any of countless other characteristics that some people dislike or look down on without rational cause.

Fortunately, you don't have to deal with everyone on the planet who holds a prejudice against you. In the context of difficult people, you need to get your head around your boss, neighbour, sister-in-law, colleague, classmate or whoever you have to interact with regularly.

Prejudice comes from ignorance. Anyone who actually knows lots of black people, say, can't help but recognise that the colour of their skin (and its effect on their history) is the only thing that sets them apart from everyone else. Otherwise they're just more people in all our infinite variety. Those who are prejudiced against other people are largely those who haven't had enough experience to recalibrate their beliefs about them.

Prejudice is often learnt from our family or culture. And then compounded by ignorance. And, of course, if you're raised to believe that a certain type of person is anything from evil to simply 'not our type', you'll most likely avoid them. Which perpetuates the ignorance. This is often fuelled by fear, that the people the prejudice is aimed at will take your job or break into your house or corrupt your children.

Most people, if confronted with the reality, will recognise that their fears and prejudices are unfounded. But certain people continue to be difficult to deal with because they refuse to see any evidence that opposes their existing beliefs. So your problem is having to deal with a boss who is convinced that women can't do the job as well as men, or the neighbour who thinks all gays are evil, or the family member who can't cope with the fact that their relative has married a black person.

The first thing is to recognise that their prejudice says a great deal about them and nothing about you. It may not feel like it, but that is obvious to everyone else around them. This in itself should help you not to take it to heart.

It also makes sense not to feed their false beliefs. If your male boss thinks women are too needy and emotional, do your very best not to burst into tears in front him, or keep asking for help (if you're a woman). Consider it your task to stand up for all women who encounter him in the future.

The thing that will reduce prejudice is experience. Not reasoned argument. Prejudice is not a logical state, so logic won't defeat it. If you challenge people overtly, they become more entrenched. Political protest on a public scale can be very effective, but on a one-to-one level provoking any kind of defensive reaction is always going to be counter-productive. Yes, regardless that you're right. Don't try to change them all at once – just plant a seed.

Your boss might eventually concede that women generally are emotional and needy but you're an exception. It's not the outcome you really want, but you've started something. The next woman who works for him, and the next, can slowly help that seed grow. It shouldn't have to take a long time but it probably will. Very few people change their beliefs overnight. So don't ask for the moon, and remember that this isn't about you.

> # THEIR PREJUDICE SAYS A GREAT DEAL ABOUT THEM AND NOTHING ABOUT YOU

Martyrs crave recognition

Being a martyr is quite like sulking, really, except that normally when someone sulks they go away and do it privately. That's sort of the point. Martyrs like to sulk in public, and draw attention to it. Then they make sure you know that they're suffering, and often that it's your fault.

There are lots of things that cause martyrs to feel bitter. Their own low self-esteem, or the fact they feel undervalued. Maybe it *is* your fault, I wouldn't know. The point is that they are resentful because, in their eyes, they are not getting the recognition they deserve. And instead of just asking for it (and here's the 'difficult' bit), something in them responds by making complaints and veiled criticisms directed at whoever they consider has failed to give them their due.

Now, the really grown-up thing to do if you feel you're not being valued is to talk to the person who you think is taking you for granted. Explain to them how you feel, and why. But martyrs don't do this. They sigh a lot and drop heavy hints and wait for you to tell them how wonderful they are. Either you'll do that just to dissipate the bad atmosphere (but you're rewarding the martyr behaviour), or you won't, in which case the mood will deteriorate.

If you're dealing with an occasional but frustrating martyr, your best bet is to do the grown-up bit for them. Say, 'I'm getting the impression you're not happy about this' to get a conversation going about why completing this piece of paperwork for the team, or doing the washing up, is making them resentful. Maybe they have a point. If they really don't, at least you've checked with them and you can move on (even if they can't).

Some people, however, routinely create martyr scenarios for themselves in order to try to boost their self-esteem by encouraging others to make expressions of appreciation. So they routinely complain about how hard they work, how badly they've been treated, how terrible their situation is, in order that you (or someone) will tell them how wonderful they are to cope with it all. Sometimes they may even take a job with long hours in order to have something to moan about (unconsciously, mind you: they won't realise that's what they've done). In this case, giving them the response they crave just feeds their addiction. This is a form of emotional blackmail, and this person is making you responsible for their self-esteem.

However sympathetic you are, this is a job for a trained therapist of some kind. Meantime, if you can't avoid this person, just keep your interactions neutral. If they tell you how late they worked last night, don't praise or sympathise. Just comment on last night's weather or something. Don't accept 'sacrifices' from them such as offers to do some of your work for you. Tell them you don't need any help.

An extreme and persistent martyr is almost certainly unhappy, but not in ways that you can do anything about (unless you're a trained psychotherapist).[24] All you can do is protect yourself, and resist feeding their appetite for praise and sympathy. If you really feel the urge to do anything beyond that, try to encourage them to seek help.

> # GIVING THEM THE RESPONSE THEY CRAVE JUST FEEDS THEIR ADDICTION

---

[24] In which case why do you need to read this?

Sensitive people can't toughen up

I once worked with a guy who would tear up at the slightest thing. The faintest hint of criticism from one of the team, a sad story on the news, any kind of negative emotion in the room. Some of us found it quite tricky being around him at times – if we needed to give him constructive feedback, it was like walking on eggshells.

If you're not highly sensitive yourself, it can be hard coping with someone who is. That's why I've included oversensitive people in this section on difficult people – because they might be difficult for you to handle. However, unlike most of the other characters in this section, oversensitive people haven't done anything wrong. They were probably born this way, and the rest of us need to learn to accommodate them. After all, they're often the first to sense trouble brewing, and can be the best diplomats because they're so highly attuned to not upsetting people. If they treat others as they'd like to be treated, there's little danger of them causing ill-feeling. It's no use telling them to 'toughen up'. They can't, and they shouldn't have to, anyway.

The problem is – especially if you're not as thin-skinned as they are – that you might upset them. Well, yes, you might. So you need to be careful. First off, recognise that the tiniest criticism can be taken to heart and dwelt on for ages. On the plus side, however, this means that you don't need to use a sledgehammer to get your point across. You can be confident that these people will pick up on hints and understatement, so just be kind and considerate.

Obviously you need to be able to tell them when their work isn't up to scratch, or things aren't going well in your relationship with them. Assuming they are not also an emotional blackmailer, their tears aren't intended to make you feel bad. They're just an uncontrollable reaction. Do your best to get them to identify problems themselves – 'There's scope for improvement here. What do you think could speed the process up next time?'. That way they can do the criticising and you can just agree.

Notice in that example how the wording was impersonal too. Not 'What could you do to speed things up?' but 'What could speed things up?'. This makes it easier to avoid any sense of personal criticism. If your partner is oversensitive, you might say, 'I feel frustrated when I go to start the car and find it's out of petrol' rather than '...when you leave the car out of petrol'.

If you're dealing with a very sensitive person, focus on the positive and use carrots rather than sticks. Sticks can be quite a scary proposition. So let them know what you want and not what you don't. You want the car to have some petrol left in it, for instance, rather than you *don't* want to find it empty.

I remember a primary school teacher once telling me he had 'a list of children not to shout at', because they couldn't take it. I concluded that he must therefore – if only by default – have a list of children to shout at. Whether or not you need a list of people to shout at (of course, you wouldn't really shout at them – you're a Rules player), the oversensitive people should definitely be on your list of people to avoid if you're feeling crabby and irascible.

> # THE TINIEST CRITICISM CAN BE TAKEN TO HEART AND DWELT ON FOR AGES

People will listen if it's in their interest

I know a couple who almost never argue or bicker. When they occasionally do, it's always about the same thing – he says she doesn't listen to him. This is quite true, she often doesn't. And I know why. It's because he repeats himself, so it's boring to listen and she switches off. Ah, but why does he repeat himself? I can tell you that too. It's because she never seems to be listening.

It takes two people co-operating for one of them to listen. Now, in the case above, I'd say it's a 50/50 split as to who is responsible for the not listening. Sometimes you'll find yourself up against someone who is contributing a lot more than 50 per cent of the problem. But it's very rare that it comes entirely from the listener's side. Even if they've got their fingers in their ears and are singing 'La, la, la . . .', there's probably a reason why they're doing that.

If someone persistently doesn't listen – or doesn't hear what you're saying – you need to do something different. Otherwise nothing will change. There will be a reason they're not listening, so work out what it is. Are you undermining their authority, criticising them, saying something they don't want to hear, making them look bad in front of someone else? Whatever the reason, try to accommodate it. Take a different tone, speak to them in private, plan out how to get your point across more succinctly, pick a better time. Show them why what you have to say is worth listening to.

Anyone is more likely to listen to you if they're on your side. So adopt a non-combative tone, pick your moment, use words that make them feel good about themselves. Even if you have to criticise (do you, do you really?), find a positive way to express it. Why should they listen unless you make it worth their while?

A note here about teenage children (now why would they crop up in a Rule about people who won't listen?). If they're simply not going to hear you, there's no point saying whatever it is. It doesn't matter how important you think it is, there's still no point. If you can't get them on your side – even using any of the Rules in the last section – let it go.

If the other person is part of the conversation, they'll find it much harder not to hear what you're saying. So ask them questions, agree with any responses you can and, most important of all (drum roll here, please), listen to what they're saying. Yep, be absolutely sure that you're not guilty of the exact same thing you're accusing them of. It's easily done. Maybe they might change your mind? No? If that's simply not possible, you're being as closed-minded as they are.

THERE WILL BE A REASON THEY'RE NOT LISTENING, SO WORK OUT WHAT IT IS

RULE 92

Passive-aggressive people fear conflict

I remember coming home very late at night as a teenager once. An elderly relative was visiting, and next morning over breakfast she said, 'I hope you had a good night last night? It can't have been bad considering you were out until 2.20am.' This was expressed to sound enthusiastic and pleased for me, but I knew perfectly well what the subtext was. She was really saying – in front of my mother – 'You woke me up when you came in.' That's how she knew what time it was.

The aim of passive-aggressive behaviour is to criticise or complain but without provoking direct conflict. We all do it occasionally, but some people default to it when they're frustrated or angry. Generally these people are afraid of conflict, usually because of bad experiences in the past, but they don't want to let their frustrations pass without comment. It's a supremely pointless form of behaviour actually, because it doesn't get their problem addressed. It just makes everyone feel uncomfortable.

I worked with someone once who used to deliver every piece of work at the last possible moment in order to make everyone else's job harder. He was never technically past the deadline, but the rest of the team always aimed to help each other by handing over tasks as soon as possible. This guy was angry at the rest of the team and this was his way of punishing us. He couldn't sit us down and say he had a problem, because he was afraid of provoking an aggressive reaction from us. I still have no idea why he was angry with us, and whatever it was it never got resolved. I expect he's still angry with whoever he works with today.

One of the big frustrations with this behaviour is that if you challenge it directly, the other person can deny it. 'But I didn't run up to the line on purpose! It just took longer than I thought.'

Hey, look, now you're the unreasonable one accusing them unfairly. And they get to be aggrieved and wronged.

So what are you going to do about your passive-aggressive boss, partner, mother, colleague, child? For a start, acknowledge to yourself that this is aggressive behaviour, however well camouflaged. This is a vital step to resisting the guilt you might otherwise feel at 'wrongly' accusing them. You help no one if you allow the aggression to continue.

Sometimes humour can work. In our family, any behaviour of this kind is likely to be met with a jokey, 'Don't get all passive-aggressive on me!' Even if the other person denies it, it's well-nigh impossible for them to continue the behaviour after that. For more persistent offenders, you need to tackle them head-on. But show them that expressing frustration doesn't have to cause conflict. That's what they fear, and they won't change their approach unless that fear recedes. So be matter-of-fact and show you want a win/win resolution to whatever's bothering them.

You'll need to be specific too. No good saying, 'You always deliver everything as late as possible.' Cite individual instances, and let them know it isn't acceptable. On no account start any kind of tit-for-tat petty retaliation, like delivering stuff to them late in return. That would make you more passive-aggressive than them. Now, where did that moral high ground go?

ACKNOWLEDGE TO YOURSELF THAT THIS IS AGGRESSIVE BEHAVIOUR, HOWEVER WELL CAMOUFLAGED

Patronising can be accidental

People who patronise often come from the same place as bullies – they put you down in order to big themselves up. They are insecure and plagued with self-doubt, and they deal with it by trying to cement your position lower down the social, intellectual or corporate ladder than they are.

As with so many kinds of difficult behaviour, this is about them and not you, and your best bet is to stay calm and politely but firmly draw attention to what they're saying: 'Why do you say I wouldn't understand? Would you like me to explain it for you?'. In front of other people, this can be very effective because it makes them feel so uncomfortable they'll think twice about doing it again.

One thing to look out for is that you aren't encouraging this behaviour. I have known people who complain about being treated as if they're incompetent, for example, and yet whenever they're given a task, they ask constantly for reassurance they're doing it properly. If this is you, it's not that surprising if some people question whether you're up to the job. They should find a better way to express this concern than by patronising you – nevertheless if you behaved more confidently, they'd stop casting aspersions on your competence.

Not everyone who patronises you, however, is doing it deliberately. Generally speaking, if it's not deliberate, it will be disguised as either kindness or praise. So someone helping you across the road is great if you need help, but can be patronising if you don't. It comes from a place of kindness though, so it's best responded to gently: 'I can manage, thank you, but I appreciate the offer.' After all, you don't want to put them off offering to help the next person, who might actually need it.

If you are older, or young, or disabled, or a woman, people some-times patronise you by speaking to your companion instead of you. It's the companion who needs to be onside here, and can keep referring questions back to you so that you speak for your-self. (They may need reminding.)

And a classic way of patronising someone is to praise them for something that doesn't warrant it. I have to say a lot of women do this when they say to their partner, 'Well done for replacing the old loo roll/vacuuming round/bathing the baby'. The implication here is that they are surprised their men were capable – which is deeply patronising. They wouldn't expect to be praised for doing the same thing.

Sexist men can do the exactly the same thing to women, offering praise for executing a three-point turn successfully, or changing a light bulb, or closing a deal. Lots of things warrant praise, but unwarranted praise is just patronising. Try asking the person if they think it's difficult – it should make them think about what they're doing, and may draw their attention to how irrational it is to praise you. If that doesn't work, you'll need to change their perception of you through experience. It takes time, but in the end they'll learn it's normal for you to operate a vacuum cleaner or point a car in another direction.

> # A CLASSIC WAY OF PATRONISING SOMEONE IS TO PRAISE THEM FOR SOMETHING THAT DOESN'T WARRANT IT

You can't beat
a true narcissist

We all know them, they're pretty easy to spot and you could prob-ably name a few with little trouble. These are those people for whom the universe revolves. And they must be at the centre, the figure of worship, never wrong, admired by everyone, always on top.

Yup, narcissists can only see things in relation to the effect on them. This blinds them to much in the way of empathy, so they struggle even to switch into considering other people – you, for example – because they're often just not interested in anything that doesn't have positive repercussions for them.

A self-focused partner or boss can be very tough to live with. Like bullies (they often are bullies), they don't necessarily have the inner confidence their behaviour implies. So they may need to put you down in order to build themselves up. They aren't interested in what they can do for you, only in what you can do for them. They are infuriatingly arrogant, and don't want to listen to you. Why would they? Clearly, they know best and you should be listening to them.

These people aren't just big personalities. They need to be right, and like you only if you agree with them and help to inflate their opinion of themselves. Lots of people you might describe as hav-ing plenty of ego can still listen, and can accept being disagreed with – some even welcome it. But your narcissist can't deal with criticism at all, and is intolerant of anyone who doesn't share their views and opinions and values. They'll take it as a personal affront.

Your best bet with these people (if you can't avoid them, which is usually the first choice) is to be clear and unemotional – they're not interested in your emotions, so don't bother troubling a nar-cissist with them. Try to be unequivocal when you deal with them: if you keep saying 'maybe', or 'I wonder if', or 'I feel' or 'I sort of', you're just undermining your authority in their eyes. And don't waste your time arguing with them. They can't allow themselves to lose an argument, so just back off or avoid it in the first place, and find a cannier way to get what you want. Preferably one that feeds their ego – that's the route to getting them to co-operate.

Retaliating by trying to put them down, or call them out in front of other people, or challenge their egotistical behaviour, is doomed to failure. However justified you might think you are – and you might be right – they won't stand for it. Belittling is what they fear most and they'll get you back for it. And they'll win, because it matters to them more than it does to you.

Mind you, a true narcissist – someone who could be clinically diagnosed as such – is far more scary. Even psychiatrists struggle to do more than scratch the surface of their behaviour. Their focus on themselves is so strong that, where necessary (to them), they will blur the line between fact and fiction to preserve their perception of themselves as being supremely successful, powerful, unique and entitled. They see themselves as being superior to the rest of us and therefore deserving of special treatment, rule bending and adulation.

If you are close to one of these people and struggling to cope, don't imagine you can change them because you can't. Just protect yourself and hold on to your own dignity and self-worth. If you are unable to live with them, your only option is to put as much space between you as necessary for you to be able to cope. Good luck.

> # THEY AREN'T INTERESTED IN WHAT THEY CAN DO FOR YOU, ONLY IN WHAT YOU CAN DO FOR THEM

Moaners don't want to change

I have a feeling I'm particularly intolerant of people who moan and whinge. It drives me round the bend. It's the negative, glass half empty thing, with which I can sympathise fully until someone persistently pours it over me.

I'll tell you what really frustrates me about it. It's the fact that while someone is focused on moaning and complaining, they're not getting on with doing something about it. We can all have a quick moan about things and then get on and make the best of it. The people I'm talking about here are the ones who do the moaning a bit like a stuck record and never progress to the sorting it out stage. So in fact they're making the whole situation worse by failing to resolve it. Almost every tricky scenario can be improved – if not entirely resolved – but only if you take action. Moaners couple their complaining with inaction.

Obviously complainers can be useful in bringing problems to your attention – like negative people (of whom they are a subset), they sometimes speak for the team or the family or the group, and can be the first to alert you to a problem that needs addressing.

However, moaners don't want to use their initiative to make things better. They want you to sort everything out, rather like a child – indeed they may still be a child, in which case your job as a parent is to encourage them to find solutions instead of just complaining. Before they grow up to inflict their whingeing on anyone else.

Looking back over years of jobs and friends, I can't recall a complainer who really embraced the concept of change. Moaners don't like change, and that's often at the root of their whingeing. They resist it, which is why they don't want to proceed to the problem-solving stage, because that would require them to accept some kind of new or adapted approach. That's not what they want.

So the way to cope with a complainer is partly to reassure them about the change – it's not so bad or so big as it looks; or see how it's going to make life better, simpler, easier – and give them a moment for this to sink in. Longer if it's a big change. If you're telling the kids that you're moving house, don't expect them to absorb it in half an afternoon.

Then get them to focus on the solution. Never mind repeating why they don't like it, 'What are you going to do about it?'. Or get them to visualise and buy into it: 'Your new bedroom will be bigger than this one, and we'll need to decide what colour to decorate it.' Get them to take a stake in the solution if you can.

Moaners often feel disenfranchised – in companies they are frequently the ones who view their team as a second family and protect it fiercely. If it's changed from above (as they see it), they feel powerless to protect it. So getting them to accept an active role in the process – whether it's restructuring the department or just moving the stationery cupboard further down the corridor – will reassure them. As well as, hopefully, shutting them up.

> # GET THEM TO FOCUS ON THE SOLUTION

Competitive complainers don't just need a whinge

While we're on the subject of moaners and complainers, here's a group of tricky people who appear to be moaners but are actually up to something else. Ever heard a conversation like this?

> A: I didn't get home until 10pm last night.
> B: Yeah, tell me about it...I wasn't home until 10.30 on Monday.
> A: I'd been in since 8am too.
> B: I've had to come in at 8am every day this week.
> A: Yeah, but I was completely shattered because I'd done three hours of driving between branch offices too.

And so on. Competitive complainers. My favourite example is the Monty Python sketch about the bunch of old guys competing over who had the toughest childhood ('I was brought up in a paper bag in the middle of the road...'). Yes, these people are complaining, but their motivation is not the same as that of the persistent moaners who were so irritating me in the last Rule.

Oh no. These people are martyrs under a different guise. This time they're dragging other people down with them. They want everyone to know how hard they work, how much they suffer, and how unappreciated they are. And like any other martyrs, they'll get worse if you reward them by sympathising (go back and re-read Rule 89 if it helps). Just ignore them and move on.

Obviously martyrs and competitive complainers are still capable of doing things well, and they deserve praise or recognition when they do. But don't link it to the martyr behaviour. Make sure you catch them when they're not complaining to tell them how pleased you are with them.

This is a particularly common behaviour between siblings – no surprises there – who are in part also competing for parental attention. So do a regular quick mental check to make sure you are distributing your time, praise, rewards and approval fairly. You very possibly are, mind you – this is about perception, which doesn't have to tally with reality. If so, reassure your complaining child, but not when they're complaining.

Actually it's easy for some people to get sucked into these competitions without ever initiating them. And that's interesting too. Apart from the once-in-a-blue-moon competitors, there is a category of people who don't start the moaning, but often pick up on it and get into a tit-for-tat competition. These are the people who wouldn't normally dream of complaining, but can't quite allow someone else to be seen to suffer more than them. So these people may genuinely deserve and need more recognition than they routinely get. Worth thinking about anyway – if they're not martyrs but silent sufferers, you can safely acknowledge their value without perpetuating negative behaviour.

THEIR MOTIVATION IS NOT THE
SAME AS THAT OF THE
PERSISTENT MOANERS

Secrets are full of power

Lots of people are quite private, and that's fair enough. No one has to discuss their personal life with their colleagues, or their deepest emotions with their family. Plenty of people are very open, while plenty choose to keep more of the details to themselves. Maybe they're shy, or vulnerable, or anxious about being judged in some way. Or maybe they're quite simply private people. Whichever is the case, I wouldn't include them here because this section is about difficult people.

So who are the *difficult* secretive people? Well, they're the ones who deliberately withhold information from you. Generally speaking, this isn't information that you know they have, so you can't be sure they're doing it. Maybe you know there's something they're not telling you but you have no idea what it is. However, they know perfectly well that they have information you want, and they're choosing not to pass it on.

Why do they do this? Because it gives them power. If they let you know they have the information, you will be complicit in this power they hold over you. If they don't tell you, they're still excited by it. And it may give them valuable knowledge that they can use. For example, a controlling partner might learn that you've done something they can hold against you (rightly or wrongly), but hang on to their secret knowledge until they can deploy it to their best advantage. Or a colleague might know that a new role is coming up that you'll want to apply for, but not tell you in order to give themselves or someone else an advantage. Or even just to disadvantage you.

One obvious example of this is people who have affairs. An affair – for them – is a huge delicious secret. Knowing something no one else does can be intoxicatingly exciting. Just having information someone else would want feels powerful. They can do anything and get away with it, because no one knows it's happening.

Of course, as in all these examples, secretive people undermine your trust in them. That can be difficult in itself because you want to be able to trust your friends, family, colleagues, boss. So what can you do?

What you *can't* do is prise the secrets out of these people. As soon as you try, you acknowledge their power and thereby increase it. You play into their hands, and if they divulge the thing, they've immediately given up their power. They're not going to do that in a hurry.

However, their power comes from having information you want. So don't ever let them see that you want it. Once you've identified a regular secret-keeper, don't trust them, and exclude them from your calculations. Get your information elsewhere. Ignore any clues they drop. If you can make them feel their power is illusory, and actually they have nothing you want, you've removed their motivation. And, crucially, you'll stop caring what they might know. You might not change their inherently secretive nature, but you'll remove its power to trouble you.

> # YOU KNOW THERE'S SOMETHING THEY'RE NOT TELLING YOU BUT YOU HAVE NO IDEA WHAT IT IS

RULE 98

Some people just can't lose

One of my friends claims he can barely stand to be around his own brother, because his brother turns everything into a competition: who has the best-paid job, the most expensive car, the most valuable house, the most exotic holidays. As you can see, in his brother's case it's all about money.

Other people are competitive about sport or shared hobbies ('What kind of camera have *you* got?' 'I've got a more specialist model train than you . . .'). Or parenting. Ooh, that's a thing. A big thing. Whose child was toilet-trained first, or got the best grades, or had the best part in the school play.

It's not just about bragging for these overly competitive people – not only must they do well, but they also need you to do less well. That's what sets it apart from mere boastfulness.

Of course, there's a reason for it. Generally, these people, when young, were given more praise or recognition or adulation for winning than they were given for, say, working hard or for being good losers. The really unlucky ones were actively chastised for failing to win or come top. In some cases their parents – and to some extent teachers – focused specifically on sport or exam grades or career success. (You and I know that career success needn't have anything to do with money, but parents busy raising over-competitive kids generally think it does.) Sometimes they just weren't allowed to come second at anything.

All of which means that it's nothing to do with you, so don't take it personally. As with so many difficult behaviours, it's all about them. Its effect on you is important, however. You consider them difficult because you dislike having to cope with their extreme competitiveness. Why is that? Do they make you feel inadequate? Are you tempted to join in to prove you have equal value?

Well, that stuff is about you – your reaction is a big part of the problem.

Listen, I'm not saying it's your fault. If someone else is taking competition to an obnoxious level, you're certainly not to blame. Your ability to cope with it might be improved, however, if you had the confidence to let it go, laugh it off, feel sorry for them. Or if you're tempted to join in and get really competitive, maybe you suffered from some of the same warped values as a child. In which case learning to recognise this and recalibrate your values will be hard, but you'll be happier for it.

Personally, I do have a favourite way of dealing with these people. It might not work for everyone but it works for me. I become inversely competitive – I try to come last in the competition: 'My child is already potty trained at 18 months...' 'Really? I wasn't planning to start mine before they're at least two.' It's not difficult with these people, and it tends to shut them up. What's more they think they've won, and I know I have – it's my private way of enjoying it instead of being riled by it. Keeps me happy.

> NOT ONLY MUST THEY DO
> WELL, BUT THEY ALSO NEED
> YOU TO DO LESS WELL

Manipulation is more than just persuasion

Extreme competitiveness, such as in the last Rule, can be one of the reasons why people become extremely sneaky and manipulative to get what they want. Of course, we can all be manipulative at times, but some people can be relied on to be sneaky and underhand as a first port of call.

I'm acutely aware that about a quarter of this book is about getting people on your side, and you could argue that's a form of manipulation. My defence is that I advocate using behaviour which doesn't disadvantage – and indeed often benefits – the other person. I'd call that influencing, not manipulating. As you know, I'm only passing on my observations of what works. However, it's fair to say that some underhand approaches can sometimes work too. But when I talk about being manipulative, I'm really talking about using stratagems and ploys which take no account of the effect on the other person, and are often to their detriment.

Right, having got that disclaimer out of the way, what is going on with these manipulators? It would be impossible to list the potential – and often complex – causes of this kind of behaviour. The key thing is that these people have been conditioned by experience to believe that this is the best way to get what they want. And good manipulators, with plenty of experience, probably are getting what they want a lot of the time. The problem is that it can be very much not what *you* want.

These people have found a novel way of controlling you, whether it's at work or in a relationship. You know they're doing it, but you can't prove it. They'll deny it, and they're often too good at it for you to feel that your boss or colleagues will believe you. They ask leading questions, they emotionally blackmail, they never accept blame, they try to convince you that you're the one with the problem, they lie, they plant false information (literally, or in people's minds), they deliberately thwart you, they have an instinct for your weak spots…A small-time manipulator is hard enough to deal with. A big-league player is a nightmare.

So how do you deal with them? For a start, don't let them convince you that it's your fault. You *know* this person is manipulative, so any suggestion that you're being over-sensitive or forgetful or unreasonable counts for nothing. Learn to believe in your own take on the situation, and not theirs. Every manipulator has their own pet strategies – think through how to recognise them and plan your responses in advance. If they claim credit from you at work, start copying the boss in on emails that show otherwise (you can say you're keeping them in the loop on a project). If they try to put words in your mouth ('Don't you think it's better for the kids to go to bed earlier?', 'Isn't that what you wanted?'), don't get sucked in. Make it clear they're expressing their view, and you'll express yours.

Learn to say no to people who cajole or play on your emotions. Don't justify yourself – you don't have to. And ultimately, if you can, avoid manipulators like the plague.

> # LEARN TO BELIEVE IN YOUR OWN TAKE ON THE SITUATION, AND NOT THEIRS

RULE 100

Busy people are less trouble

If your boss is particularly difficult, it can be hard to distract them – but you'll probably have noticed that they're easier to deal with when they're pre-occupied elsewhere, if only because you encounter them a bit less often. However, for just about everyone else, one of the keys to coping is to find them something to do.

This works on several levels. First off, a project of some kind gives them something to focus on other than winding you up. You need to find them a relatively autonomous job, where they're out of the way of the people they might otherwise antagonise. So if you're planning a big family holiday together, you might ask your sister-in-law to take charge of all the travel arrangements, or researching and booking the accommodation. Even if you're not in charge, you can recommend her: 'Hey, I think Ali would be brilliant at organising the travel. Ali, you're so organised and we don't want to risk any last-minute crises with so many of us going.'

Think carefully about the right role – if you put her in charge of food in a self-catering place, she could drive everyone mad telling them when they're on shopping/cooking/washing-up duty. It depends what her particular skills are and in what way she's hard to deal with (and whether it's just you, or whether the whole family find her frustrating).

Where it's useful, you can ease things further by finding a job that puts some physical distance between the tricky person and anyone else who needs a break from them. You know, send someone off to research something, or go and visit potential venues or something.

For another thing, whatever it is that makes someone difficult, they'll be easier if they feel valued than if they feel rejected. Suppose you're running a team at work and there's a big exhibition coming up. If you have a difficult team member and you try to keep them at arm's length, they're going to feel excluded and frustrated. That's not going to help. Whereas if you make them responsible for planning and organising all the materials to go on the stand, they'll feel important and appreciated. And that's got to be a less bad option. Make sure they know you've given them that role because they're really reliable/so experienced/a terrific organiser/ have a great eye for detail. Let them take pride in doing a good job, because that will make everyone's lives easier.

This has another advantage too, because now the rest of the team, family, group or whoever, is going to feel happier for having a bit of space between themselves and their difficult colleague/relative/ friend. So they'll work better and the team will be more cohesive.

And once the difficult person has been a successful (if pre-occupied) part of a team once, they're that bit more likely to make things work next time. If you're their boss, you can use it as a positive experience when you're working through their people skills with them. If you're their sister-in-law, maybe you've found them a niche as the family travel organiser in future, where they can do a good job and everyone else can relax more easily.

> # A PROJECT GIVES THEM SOMETHING TO FOCUS ON OTHER THAN WINDING YOU UP

THESE ARE THE RULES

I have spent a lifetime watching, learning and distilling the Rules of how happy and successful people behave. I have observed what it is that these people do, and others do not. Whether it's at work or in their relationships, as parents or managing their money, I can tell you why their lives run more smoothly than other people's.

The Rules aren't orders. You don't *have* to obey them. I'm not telling you how you should live your life. I'm just passing on what I've learnt myself, in the hope you can make use of it. You'll be happier and more successful if you follow the Rules, but it's your call.

Some of these Rules – many of them – are common sense. They're a reminder, not a revelation. But somehow you need to see them in black and white to realise that you've wandered off the track. Others may take a bit longer to get your head round. And you might even disagree with a few. That's fine – you're allowed to think for yourself. In fact, it's actively encouraged.

There are eight books in the *Rules* series, to help you make a success of just about every part of your life:

The Rules of Work
The Rules of Life
The Rules of Love
The Rules of Management
The Rules of Wealth
The Rules of Parenting
The Rules of People
The Rules to Break

Richard Templar

Anybody can be wealthy — you just need to apply yourself

The lovely thing about money is that it really doesn't discriminate. It doesn't care what colour or race you are, what class you are, what your parents did, or even who you *think* you are. Each and every day starts with a clean slate so that no matter what you did yesterday, today begins anew and you have the same rights and opportunities as everyone else to take as much as you want. The only thing that can hold you back is yourself and your own money myths.

> **YOU HAVE THE SAME RIGHTS**
>
> **AND OPPORTUNITIES**
>
> **AS EVERYONE ELSE TO TAKE AS**
>
> **MUCH AS YOU WANT**

Of the wealth of the world each has as much as they take. What else could make sense? There is no way money can know who is handling it, what their qualifications are, what ambitions they have or what class they belong to. Money has no ears or eyes or senses. It is inert, inanimate, impassive. It hasn't a clue. It is there to be used and spent, saved and invested, fought over, seduced with and worked for. It has no discriminatory apparatus so it can't judge whether you are 'worthy' or not.

I have watched a lot of extremely wealthy people and the one thing they all have in common is that they have nothing in common – apart from all being Rules players of course. The wealthy are a diverse band of people – the least likely can be loaded. They vary from the genteel to the uncouth, the savvy to the plain stupid, the deserving to the undeserving. But each and every one of them has stepped up and said, 'Yes please, I want some of that'. And the poor are the ones saying, 'No thank you, not for me, I am not worthy. I am not deserving enough. I couldn't. I mustn't. I shouldn't'.

That's what this book is about, challenging your perceptions of money and the wealthy. We all assume the poor are poor because of circumstances, their background, their upbringing, their nurture. But if you have the means to buy a book such as this and live in comparative security and comfort in the world then you too have the power to be wealthy. It may be hard. It may be tough but it is doable. And that is Rule 1 – anyone can be wealthy, you just need to apply yourself. All the other Rules are about that application.

Get your work noticed

It's all too easy for your work to get overlooked in the busy hurly burly of office life. You're slaving away and it can be hard to remember that you need to put in some effort to boost your individual status and personal kudos for your work. But it's important. You have to make your mark so you stand out and your promotional potential will be realised.

The best way to do this is to step outside the normal working routine. If you have to process so many widgets each day – and so does everyone else – then processing more won't do you that much good. But if you submit a report to your boss of how everyone could process more widgets then you'll get noticed. The unsolicited report is a brilliant way to stand out from the crowd. It shows you're thinking on your feet and using your initiative. But it mustn't be used too often. If you subject your boss to a barrage of unsolicited reports, you'll get noticed but in completely the wrong way. You have to stick to certain rules:

- Only submit a report occasionally.

- Make really sure that your report will actually work – that it will do good or provide benefits.

- Make sure your name is prominently displayed.

- Make sure the report will be seen not only by your boss, but by their boss as well.

- Remember it doesn't have to be a report – it can be an article in the company newsletter.

Of course, the very best way to get your work noticed is to be very, very good at your job. And the best way to be good at your job is to be totally dedicated to doing the job and ignoring all the rest. There is a vast amount of politics, gossip, gamesmanship, time wasting and socialising that goes on in the name of work. It isn't work. Keep your eye on the ball and you'll already be playing with a vast advantage over your colleagues. The Rules player stays focused. Keep your mind on the task at hand – being very good at your job – and don't get distracted.

THE UNSOLICITED REPORT IS A BRILLIANT WAY TO STAND OUT FROM THE CROWD

Get them emotionally involved

You manage people. People who are paid to do a job. But if it is 'just a job' to them, you'll never get their best. If they come to work looking to clock in and clock off and do as little as they can get away with in between, then you're doomed to failure, my friend. On the other hand, if they come to work looking to enjoy themselves, looking to be stretched, challenged, inspired and to get involved, then you are in with a big chance of getting the very best out of them. Trouble is, the jump from drudge to super team is entirely down to you. It is you that has to inspire them, lead them, motivate them, challenge them, get them emotionally involved.

That's OK. You like a challenge yourself, don't you? The good news is that getting a team emotionally involved is easy. All you have to do is make them care about what they are doing. And that's easy too. You have to get them to see the relevance of what they are doing, how it makes an impact on people's lives, how they provide the needs of other human beings, how they can reach out and touch people by what they do at work. Get them convinced – because it is true of course – that what they do makes a difference, that it contributes to society in some way rather than just lines the owner's or shareholders' pockets, or ensures that the chief executive gets a big fat pay cheque.

And yes. I know it's easier to show how they contribute if you manage nurses rather than an advertising sales team, but if you think about it, then you can find value in any role and instil pride in those who do whatever job it is. Prove it? OK. Well, those who sell advertising space are helping other companies, some of which may be very small, reach their markets. They are alerting potential customers to things they may have wanted for a long time and may really need. They are keeping the newspaper or magazine afloat as it relies on ad sales income, and that magazine or newspaper delivers information and/or gives pleasure to the people who buy it (otherwise they wouldn't, would they?).

Get them to care because that's an easy thing to do. Look, this is a given. Everyone deep down wants to be valued and to be useful. The cynics will say this is nonsense, but it is true, deep down true. All you have to do is reach down far enough and you will find care, feeling, concern, responsibility and involvement. Drag all that stuff up and they'll follow you forever and not even realise why.

Oh, just make sure that you've convinced yourself first before you try this out on your team. Do you believe that what you do makes a positive difference? If you're not sure, reach down, deep down, and find a way of caring...

> ## GET THEM CONVINCED – BECAUSE IT IS TRUE OF COURSE – THAT WHAT THEY DO MAKES A DIFFERENCE

Relax

So who are the best parents you know? The ones who have a seemingly instinctive ability to say and do the things that will result in happy, confident, well-balanced children? Have you ever wondered what makes them so good at it? Now think about the ones you privately don't think are much cop. Why not?

All the best parents I know have one key thing in common. They're relaxed about it. And all the worst ones are hung up on something. Maybe they're not stressed out about how good they are as parents (perhaps they should be) but they're hung up about something that affects their ability to be a really good parent.

I know a couple of parents who are neurotically clean and tidy. Their children have to take their shoes off at the door or the whole world falls apart. Even if the shoes are clean. They get really uptight if their children leave anything out of place or make any kind of a mess (even if it gets cleared up later). It makes it impossible for the kids just to relax and enjoy themselves, in case they get grass stains on their trousers, or knock over the ketchup bottle.

I have another friend who is so obsessively competitive that his children are under huge pressure to win every friendly game they ever play. And one who frets excessively every time her child grazes his knees. I bet you can think of plenty of similar examples among people you know.

The really good parents I've encountered, on the other hand, expect their children to be noisy, messy, bouncy, squabbly, whingy and covered in mud. They take it all in their stride. They know they've got 18 years to turn these small creatures into respectable grown-ups, and they pace themselves. No rush to get them acting like adults – they'll get there in good time.

Between you and me, this Rule gets easier with time, though some people still never master it the way true Rules parents do. It's much harder to relax fully with your first baby than with your last teenager to leave home. With babies, you need to focus on the essentials – a healthy baby that isn't too hungry or too uncomfortable – and don't sweat the rest of it. It doesn't matter if their poppers are done up wrong, or you didn't find time to bath them today, or you've gone away for the weekend without anything for them to sleep in (yes, I have a friend who has done this, and no, she didn't sweat it, being a Rules parent).

Much better altogether if you can get to the end of each day, put your feet up with a glass of wine or a G&T,* and say cheerfully to each other, 'What the hell... they're all still alive so we must have got something right'.

REALLY GOOD PARENTS EXPECT THEIR CHILDREN TO BE NOISY, MESSY, BOUNCY, SQUABBLY, WHINGY AND COVERED IN MUD

---

* No, I'm not encouraging parents to use alcohol to get them through. Just relax!

Be yourself

Isn't it just so tempting to reinvent yourself when you meet somebody new who you really fancy? Or to try and be who you think they are looking for? You could become really sophisticated, or maybe strong and silent and mysterious. At least you could stop embarrassing yourself by making jokes at inappropriate moments, or being pathetic about coping with problems.

Actually, no you couldn't. At least, you might manage it for an evening or two, or even a month or two, but it's going to be tough keeping it up forever. And if you think this person is the one – you know, the one – then you might be spending the next half century or so with them. Just imagine, 50 years of pretending to be sophisticated, or suppressing your natural sense of humour.

That's not going to happen, is it? And would you really want a lifetime of lurking behind some sham personality you've created? Imagine how that would be, unable ever to let on that this wasn't really you at all, for fear of losing them. And suppose they find out in a few weeks' or months' or years' time, when you finally crack? They're not going to be very impressed, and nor would you be if it was them who turned out to have been acting out of character all along.

I'm not saying you shouldn't try to turn over the occasional new leaf; improve yourself a bit. We should all be doing that all the time, and not only in our love life. Sure, you can try to be a bit more organised, or less negative. Changing your behaviour is all fine and good. This Rule is about changing your basic personality. That won't work, and you'll tie yourself in knots trying to do it convincingly.

So be yourself. Might as well get it all out in the open now. And if that's not who they're looking for, at least you won't get in too deep before they find out. And you know what? Maybe they don't actually like sophisticated. Perhaps strong silent types don't do it for them. Maybe they'll love your upfront sense of humour. Perhaps they want to be with someone who needs a bit of looking after.

You see, if you fake it, you'll attract someone who belongs with a person that isn't you. And how will that help? Somewhere out there is someone who wants exactly the kind of person you are, complete with all the flaws and failings you come with. And I'll tell you something else – they won't even see them as flaws and failings. They'll see them as part of your unique charm. And they'll be right.

> # MIGHT AS WELL GET IT ALL OUT
> # IN THE OPEN NOW

You'll get older but not necessarily wiser

There is an assumption that as we get older we will get wiser; not true I'm afraid. The rule is we carry on being just as daft, still making plenty of mistakes. It's just that we make new ones, different ones. We do learn from experience and may not make the same mistakes again, but there is a whole new pickle jar of fresh ones just lying in wait for us to trip up and fall into. The secret is to accept this and not to beat yourself up when you do make new ones. The Rule really is: be kind to yourself when you do muck things up. Be forgiving and accept that it's all part of that growing older but no wiser routine.

Looking back, we can always see the mistakes we made, but we fail to see the ones looming up. Wisdom isn't about not making mistakes, but about learning to escape afterwards with our dignity and sanity intact.

When we are young, ageing seems to be something that happens to, well, old people. But it does happen to us all and we have no choice but to embrace it and roll with it. Whatever we do and whoever we are, the fact is we are going to get older. And this ageing process does seem to speed up as we get older.

You can look at it this way – the older you get, the more areas you've covered to make mistakes in. There will always be new areas of experience where we have no guidelines and where we'll handle things badly, overreact, get it wrong. And the more flexible we are, the more adventurous, the more life-embracing, then the more new avenues there will be to explore – and make mistakes in of course.

As long as we look back and see where we went wrong and resolve not to repeat such mistakes, there is little else we need to do. Remember that any Rules that apply to you also apply to everyone else around you. They are all getting older too. And not any wiser particularly. Once you accept this, you'll be more forgiving and kinder towards yourself and others.

Finally, yes, time does heal and things do get better as you get older. After all, the more mistakes you've made, the less likely that you'll come up with new ones. The best thing is that if you get a lot of your mistakes over and done with early on in life, there will be less to learn the hard way later on. And that's what youth is all about, a chance to make all the mistakes you can and get them out of the way.

WISDOM ISN'T ABOUT NOT MAKING MISTAKES BUT ABOUT LEARNING TO ESCAPE AFTERWARDS WITH OUR DIGNITY AND SANITY INTACT